DANIEL
My Brother

Mystery in the Mojave

DOUGLAS WALKER

Copyright © 2023 by Douglas Walker

All rights reserved. No part of this publication may be reproduced, distributed, or transmitted in any form or by any means, including photocopying, recording, digital scanning, or other electronic or mechanical methods, without the prior written permission of the publisher, except in the case of brief quotations embodied in critical reviews and certain other noncommercial uses permitted by copyright law.

Published 2023

ISBN: 979-8-218-34776-5

Cover photograph by Tom Wiznerowicz

Cover and interior design by Andy Meaden meadnecreative.com

This work depicts actual events in the author's life as truthfully as recollection merits and can be verified by research and used with permission. I have changed some names and characteristics, compressed events, and recreated some dialog.

For Daniel, My Brother

I hoped your story could be told as accurately as possible. You have been steering me on this path for years, sending me messages around October 1, year after year. You disappeared quickly from our lives and left a deep void. Every old friend we contacted speaks highly of you, Dan, "always and without exception." I wrote this to try to tell your truth. No one needs to speculate anymore.

For Ken

I apologize for asking you to relive something one should only have to live through once, but it has been a pleasure getting to know you and the man you have become. You came out of it all a thoughtful, kind, and considerate human being. I hope being able to tell your story was as cathartic for you as hearing it has been for me. You had always wondered who your driver was that night. Now you know.

Contents

Prologue	1
Just Another Tuesday	5
The Good Life in The Sixties	13
Daniel My Brother	17
The Trip to Abilene and Buffalo Gap	23
Digging Through Memories	29
The Connection	43
A Long-Overdue Meeting	47
Ken Robinson	55
Down on the Bayou	67
Home	75
The Homestead and Richard Menzies	81
Whizzing Around with "Wiz"	99
The Attempt at College	109
Derrel's House	125
Getting to Cajon Pass	139
The Killers and Speculation	149

Daniel My Brother Redux	161
Why So Long	169
Europe '72	181
Back To Denver	189
Please Come to L.A.	193
Ear and Eyewitness	211
The World Tilts	225
Sunday Morning	231
Danny Boy: A Blog by Richard Menzies September 29, 2011	235
Request	239
Acknowledgments	241

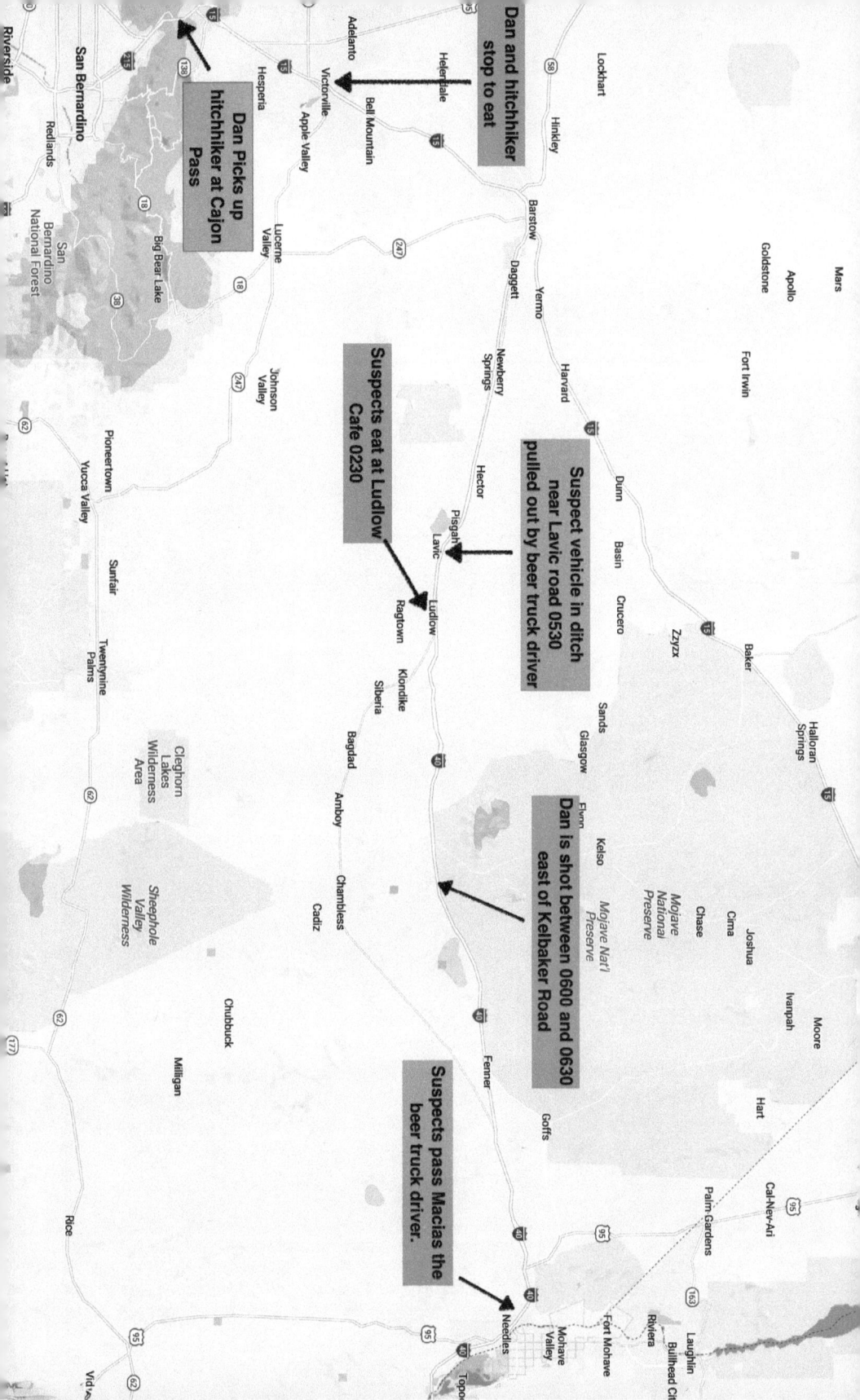

Prologue

Telling my brother's story has been a struggle for many reasons. The primary reason was there were no professional writers close enough to the events who were invested and interested in putting the words to pages. Few still alive knew the vague and now-aged facts. Those few had little interest in looking back and delving deeper into this history.

There were other resistances to exploring and documenting this history. Overcoming the family tradition of trying to forget and moving on with life was part of that resistance. My older sister is the only other person knowledgeable who could tell this story. Debbie, almost three years older than Dan and nine years older than me, adheres to that tradition. From October 1974 into the eighties and nineties, I recall only one exchange between us regarding Dan. At a wedding in 1989, during a cover of Elton John's *Daniel*, our eyes caught. We shared a sad smile and a nod across the black grand piano and gathered crowd.

Fear that some would receive the story as another late-sixties, early-seventies hippie story also impeded its telling. Dan wasn't a hippie. I believe he would have disapproved of being corralled by any label. He simply wanted to break free to see and feel as much as possible, as quickly and intensely as possible.

Until the more recent past, even those closest to the events knew only a portion of what had happened. The only details known for decades were what one could read in old letters, news articles, and police bulletins. More recent information has given the story more color, depth, and dimension.

It's no longer just about Dan.

Of those closest to this story, each has a unique view of the events and how they had unfolded, the aftermath, and the way we all folded things back up for safekeeping in the back of our minds somewhere but always uncomfortably there. Those with only limited facts and insight regarding the events of early October 1974 invented their own interpretations. More accurate information never made its way past our immediate family and Dan's closest friends. Other than my parents, especially my father, I knew more than most being a young, silent, curious observer.

Some interpretations were overly simplistic or flat-out wrong. I don't know where the rumors started. I think some had caught wind of unrelated fragments separated by time and temperament and filled in their own blanks. That happens. I heard speculation more than once that "Dan died because of drugs." I wasn't sure what that meant. Was there a belief that Dan was in some way culpable for his own death with some sort of involvement in drugs? Was it what they heard (speculated) about the motive or state of mind of the murderers? I never once questioned or pushed back at these interpretations, no matter how often over the years I had heard them. Why? I wish I could say. This is my pushback.

Hours of interviews languished in a desk drawer, ignored for years. Then in January 2019, I visited Louisiana for a family wedding. Against the backdrop of a giant Cajun celebration in Lafayette with a pirogue full of iced-down raw oysters and other regional delicacies and a band playing so loud it was hard to have a conversation, a cousin leaned into my ear and asked, "What happened to your brother?"

Michael lived north of Baton Rouge, where we had family roots. Dan and Michael were the same age. I hadn't thought about it before that moment, but they likely played together as kids before our family moved from Louisiana to Illinois. I met Michael only once before. His question didn't surprise me, even this many years after Dan's death. Not knowing exactly where to begin or what he might already know, I asked, "What did you hear happened to him?"

Michael replied, "That he was killed because of drugs."

I shook my head and tried to whisper-scream into his ear over the band's high-decibel performance, a condensed version of the facts. I tried to emphasize that it was pure chance, a simple twist of fate more than anything else, that had put Dan at that spot, that day, at that hour.

The wedding was a magnificent event. It's always wonderful to see Louisiana relatives. They do "laissez les bons temps rouler" (let the good times roll).

When I returned home to Montana, I broke out the recordings from 2010 and started writing Dan's story to the best of my ability. I had never aspired to be a writer. Dan did! He had a creative and imaginative mind. I either missed out on those genes or never tried to tap into them.

Fortunately, others in my family don't share my shortcomings. Letters saved from years back helped tell the story. Serendipity and perhaps a collective thawing of long-suppressed emotions played parts and filled forgotten or unknown gaps in Dan's history.

My older sister and I caught up over the phone in 2018. Coincidentally, it was October 1, the date of Dan's death. She said something interesting happened during her fifty-year high school class reunion that summer. One of Dan's classmates showed up and wanted to chat about Dan. Michelle and Dan were close friends in their later high school years and into college. Unfortunately for Michelle, it's a subject my sister avoids and one of the reasons it took months for Debbie to mention it to me. During their brief encounter, Michelle told Deb she had a bunch of letters from Dan she had held onto all this time. I took note.

In summer 2019, I contacted Michelle. She and her husband Bob invited me to their Diamond Lake home, a visit that was to include a cruise on their boat. I hadn't been on a boat on Diamond Lake since 1969.

It stormed with heavy rain the morning of our meeting, so the boat ride seemed like a bust. As I arrived at their home, the clouds parted, and the sun came out. Michelle and I, having never known each other, shared a tearful embrace. In her hand was a clear plastic bag filled with letters she was eager to share. She had been studying in England when she received the news about Dan.

Michelle's husband, Bob, piloted us to the southwest end of the lake and turned off the boat's engine. As we drifted, I told them Dan's story as I now knew it until we floated to the back of our old home on the lake.

Just Another Tuesday

My view as the youngest of three is that life granted us abundant opportunity and we had it good growing up, but that view is skewed and different from my sister's. She was born nine years earlier in New Orleans before our father found success selling pianos for a company based in the Chicago area.

The view I had was from two-and-a-half acres on Diamond Lake in Mundelein, Illinois, when my folks threw some out-of-control parties. They had adopted a hard-working, fast-living, party lifestyle that included excessive amounts of alcohol, not unusual for the time or among their peers. Their drinking was primarily in the spirit of fun versus coping, at least in those years.

The lifestyle on Diamond Lake was great, but our folks were living above their means until fate forced a move to a more modest property in Libertyville, the next town east, in January 1971. The party continued, but our fortunes seemed altered in the new location. Through it all, negotiating life's bumps, our parents stayed married. I like to think that despite the bumps, they also remained in love.

It was just another Tuesday. Just another day of my sophomore year. I attended classes at Carmel and, after school, football practice. I was fifteen and didn't have my license to drive. Most mornings, I grabbed the bus to school, weaving in and out of Libertyville neighborhoods for an hour before completing the journey at our Catholic high school in Mundelein.

Late that summer, early in the school year, there were rumblings that my brother would be coming home from California. I was hoping the rumblings were true, and I was also optimistic that whatever friction remained between Danny and my father had eased and that he would soon be back in town and maybe stay for a while. I really hadn't seen much of my older brother for the better part of three years. I was looking forward to having him back in my life—our lives—and hearing his travel stories. Dan's most recent location was with longtime family friends in Tustin. He had recently sent a note wishing our mother well on an upcoming medical procedure.

Health issues plagued our mother while we were growing up. They were mostly back problems resulting from, what we were told, a fall she had taken while cheerleading at Louisiana State University (LSU). At the time, doctors prescribed bed rest for orthopedic issues such as hers, which never helped her heal. Smoking, drinking, and her lifestyle didn't help either. Suffice it to say, we kids were used to Mom not feeling well. This time though, on this Tuesday, it wasn't her back—she had been admitted to the hospital for a hysterectomy.

From what I remember, my father kept a normal work schedule that day. He went down to Skokie, worked a normal day, and raced home before I arrived home from football practice. He wanted to prepare a quick meal for the two of us and drive to Lake Forest Hospital to visit Mom, whose surgery was the following morning.

Perhaps because of the events that transpired that evening, I don't recall how I got home that day just before six.

The *Andy Griffith Show* was in syndication after a great run in the Sixties. Who didn't love Andy, Opie, Aunt Bee, and the hilarious Barney

Fife? It was wholesome, funny, and imparted a few life lessons via Andy's down-home humor and fatherly wisdom.

My father was already home, rushing around preparing a meal, and getting ready to leave for the hospital when I arrived home from football practice and switched on the TV. The whistling theme of the *Andy Griffith Show* came on with a simultaneous ringing of our phone.

Hustling down the hall and into the kitchen behind me, my father picked up the receiver. While Andy and Opie whistled their way to their fishing hole, the world changed for us. The words I heard on one side of the phone conversation are forever embedded in my memory.

"Hi Bob, how are you?"

It was my father's close friend in Tustin, Bob Bull, aka Uncle Bob.

My father was quiet while Uncle Bob spoke.

"Oh, my God, Bob!" my dad cried. "Oh, my God, Bob. No! Oh, my God, Bob!"

I knew at that moment that my older brother was dead. It could be nothing else. There was nothing else.

I don't remember any more of their conversation from there. It wasn't long. I can't imagine what my dad's longtime friend was going through, delivering such awful news on the other end of the phone. At that time, the Bull family and ours had shared close ties, and our fathers had been business associates for nearly twenty-five years.

Dad hung the receiver on its hook. My back was now to Andy, Opie, and Barney. Dad looked at me with a blank stare.

"Uncle Bob said Danny is dead."

My father was pretty tough. He had endured a fair amount of adversity and had come out of it all with some success. He was a positive person. That is, up until that moment and, perhaps, never again.

"What happened?" I asked.

"Uncle Bob said he was murdered. Shot to death."

"Who would want to shoot Danny?"

"Uncle Bob knows nothing more than that Danny was shot to death after he left their house in Tustin last night."

Thinking out loud, trying to formulate a plan, Dad said, "I need to get to the hospital. Uncle Bob said we will be getting a call from authorities confirming Danny's death. I need you to be here to take the call. I'm not going to tell Mom until we get confirmation from authorities."

I remember being in awe of that decision. It was the right course, however hard it would be to pull it off in front of his wife of twenty-five-plus years. He didn't say much more to me before he left. What was there to say? His distress and confusion were plain to see. The door shut behind him, and I heard the Chevy Nova back out of the garage and leave for the hospital about twenty minutes away. I turned off the *Andy Griffith Show*.

I'm not sure if I've ever been in a home so empty. I know I paced. I paced around the first floor of the house. When I couldn't find comfort on the first floor, I went upstairs. I sat on my bed but immediately arose and paced more of the upstairs. Back down the stairs I went. I even visited the basement. The call came on my second tour of the upstairs. It couldn't have been more than fifteen minutes after my father had left. The phone upstairs was on the nightstand of my parents' bedroom.

"Hello," I answered, sitting on their bed.

The caller on the other end introduced himself and his title. I don't recall his name, but I remember the title: San Bernardino, California, County Coroner.

"Is this the residence of Daniel Ashton Walker Junior?"

"Yes."

"I want to inform you that he has been killed, and we have his body here in the coroner's building in San Bernardino. Are you able to inform other family members?"

I replied, "Yes."

The coroner said, "Thank you," and hung up.

My eyes began to tear. I paced the upstairs floor plan again, then, perhaps the first lucid thing I'd done in the last fifteen or twenty minutes, went downstairs and walked out the front door into the brisk October evening. Tears were now flowing freely, and it was hard to see. The streetlights on our street became giant, blurred stars. I raised my middle finger at the sky and shouted, "If this is your world, count me out!" I drew a couple of deep breaths, returned inside, and continued to pace.

An emotional time warp had set in, and I lost track of how much time had passed and how quickly. My father must have been gone for an hour and a half.

He arrived home, entered the house, looked at me, and asked, "Did anyone call?"

"The San Bernardino County Coroner called. Danny is dead, and they have his body."

My father, with all his faults, was a loving father. Affection toward his children came easily and often. He reached to hold me. He had never held me tighter than in that moment.

"Did you tell Mom?" I asked, crying on his shoulder.

"No, but she knew something was wrong. It was impossible to hide."

"How did you pull that off?" I was now sobbing.

He let go, tears in his eyes, too, holding my shoulders.

"I told her I was getting a horrible case of flu with diarrhea."

"You're kidding me." I shook my head, sobbing, amazed at the creativity under pressure.

"No. There was no way to hide that something was going on, so the closest thing to accurate was to say I'm really sick, and I am!"

We were on our way back to the hospital within minutes in the Nova. We barely spoke. I tried to get more details from my father, but he didn't know any more than what he'd told me. We both knew only what each other knew, which was next to nothing. Danny was dead, and his body was in a morgue in California. Our minds raced. What the hell had happened? Who would want to kill Danny? It didn't make any sense!

I couldn't say when my father informed the staff at Lake Forest Hospital, but it felt like all caring and sympathetic hands available reached out to us as we walked onto the floor and toward my mom's hospital room. I lost many details of that night and the following days in the emotional fog, but I will never forget the shocked look on my mother's face as we walked into the room and my father sat on the hospital bed beside her and grasped her hands. She knew it had to be bad news. Why was her husband back so soon? Why was I there? I tried not to watch. I turned away, but I had turned toward the room's mirror. It reflected the brutal dual view of me crying and the wrenching pain of my parents' interaction behind me. In the following moments, the hospital staff converged upon the room. The three of us exited the hospital within minutes, my mother slumped in my father's arms.

I was told to go to school the next morning.

What?

As I arrived at school the following day, a close friend met me and walked beside me but did not say much. I must have phoned him at some point.

Our sophomore football coach, Coach Scordino, was next to catch me in the hallway.

"Did you get some bad news yesterday?"

I had no idea how Coach had gotten the news so quickly. It had been barely thirteen hours since I had.

"Yes, my brother was murdered." It was surreal hearing those words come from my mouth. It was the first time I remember saying it aloud.

This was stuff you saw on television. I couldn't believe it was happening to us.

Dan had been working for a sailboat manufacturing company as a carpenter in Southern California since mid-July, living with longtime family friends my parents had known since the early fifties, the Bulls. My father and Bob Bull had become close friends working in the musical instrument business together. Our mothers came to be equally close if not closer and so did us kids. Their oldest child, David, was near in age to Dan, and he had three younger sisters. Uncle Bob and Aunt Connie, as we knew them, were very much like a second set of parents when we were growing up and had great influences in our lives. You could say the same of my parents, Uncle Dan and Aunt Lee, to the Bull children.

In the days, weeks, and months that followed, we learned that Dan had picked up a hitchhiker after he left the Bulls' home in Southern California. Dan was likely heading for Denver, but Dan's travel plans were loose. The papers reported that Dan altered his route to help the hitchhiker get to Texas quicker because his mother was in the hospital, taking Interstate 40 east from Barstow toward Arizona instead of heading north toward Nevada.

The two had stopped to rest in the middle of the Mojave Desert an hour west of Needles, California. Sometime in the early morning, two men with shotguns came up to Dan's Volkswagen van and shot Dan as he slept across the front bench seat of the van. The hitchhiker was asleep in the back, shielded from view by Dan's gear and a small motorcycle. He reportedly heard Dan plea for his life, "Man, don't shoot me!" after the first two blasts from the shotguns, and then two more shotgun blasts.

We were told the hitchhiker was instrumental (with the assistance of others) in helping get Dan to the hospital in Needles where Dan was pronounced dead. The police questioned the hitchhiker for a couple of days before clearing him of any culpability and sending him on his way. I never learned his name. I don't think my father ever got his name.

For whatever reason his name was never revealed to us, I could only speculate.

With the hitchhiker's eyewitness description of the two men and their gold GMC or Chevy van, the police tracked down a beer truck driver who believed he had helped the murderers get their vehicle unstuck from the desert sand less than an hour before they shot Dan. One assailant, the beer truck driver remembered, called the other "Sam." The beer truck driver also believed he heard them say they had just purchased the van in Whittier, California, and were heading to Indiana to hook up with an ex-wife, or girlfriend, and child of one of the two men.

As the investigation went on and law enforcement shared more information with our family, investigators told us a similar murder had occurred in Arizona off Interstate 8 near Casa Grande. It was just days after Dan's murder and approximately 350 miles southeast from where Dan was killed. This time, the victim was a highway worker out earning a living in the early morning. There were no witnesses, and I don't know whether law enforcement ever formally connected the two incidents.

For nearly two years, my father and Dan's other father, Bob Bull, kept in close touch with Detectives Forbush and May of the San Bernardino County Police Department. Still, the case soon went cold, and no solid clues or leads surfaced despite seemingly diligent efforts. The case stayed cold. We all went on with our lives, and we tried to forget.

The Good Life in The Sixties

When folks out of the know heard of Dan's death in the Mojave, far from home, I believe they made assumptions about his reasons for being in California, especially considering rumors that drugs played a role.

My father became friends with Bob Bull in 1950 when Bob and his new wife, Connie, moved to the French Quarter of New Orleans. He was beginning his career in sales at a Louisiana-based retailer of musical instruments, Werlein's Music Company. That is where Bob met my father and our grandmother, New Orleans and French Quarter natives already working in sales at Werlein's. His father had snubbed Bob for a position in the family business, Story and Clark Piano Company. His father, Perkins Bull, feared the appearance of nepotism and harbored skepticism regarding his maverick son's talent, dedication, and business acumen.

Our parents embraced the Bulls, who were from the northern suburbs of Chicago and welcomed them with open arms to the rich culture of Louisiana. They took them crabbing on the coast, and crawddadin' in the bayou. They introduced them to the great regional cuisine, and to relatives across the state.

The two families' lives would be closely intertwined for the next twenty years as Bob would become first a salesman, then a key decision-maker, and finally president at Story and Clark Piano Company. Uncle Bob recruited our father, helped the family move to Illinois, and he and Aunt Connie returned the earlier favor by being guides to a new job, latitude, and culture (Chicagoland). They were also advisers and financial backers to our parents in their first significant real estate investment.

During the bulk of the sixties, the Bulls lived on a beautiful property across the street from a small lake named Sylvan Lake. Early that decade, with financial help from the Bulls, our family moved to another wonderful home with two acres on a 150-acre lake called Diamond Lake in Mundelein, a far-north suburb of Chicago. It was a stark contrast in lifestyle from a few years earlier when my parents lived with two young children in a small shotgun apartment duplex on North Gayoso Street in New Orleans, with relatives renting the adjoining apartment.

The Bull's youngest daughter Julie and I were less than four months apart in age. When together over the years, we marveled at our lives back then. Her family in a nice home on acreage with a garden and apple orchard within yards of a lake. Ours was three miles away on another beautiful lakefront property. Being young children, we couldn't fully appreciate it, as we did when we were older.

From the time our family relocated to Illinois from Louisiana in the mid-fifties until 1970, our fathers worked together, they often traveled together on lengthy business trips across the US, and the bonds between our two families grew deeper. We spent nearly every holiday during those years with our friends the Bulls. Thanksgiving, Fourth of July, and Labor Day at the Bulls. Christmas, Easter, and Memorial Day at the Walkers. Though unrelated by blood, we shared familial traditions, and we have the memories.

In the late sixties, the musical instrument business matured, and another company acquired Story and Clark. While our father remained at the newly formed organization, Uncle Bob, after fulfilling contractual obligations, quit, moved his family to Memphis, and became CEO at another musical instrument company. After a year, frustrated with his inability to change the culture of his new company, he attempted early retirement and moved the family to Midway, Utah, where he and Aunt Connie had invested with family in a seasonal resort called The Homestead. Aunt Connie's parents, Ferrin and Martha Whitaker, had managed The Homestead for years and were the other majority owners.

After wintering over a year in Utah, still in their forties, and with Aunt Connie's growing restlessness in the small town of Midway, Uncle Bob accepted a position with CBS as an officer in their musical instrument division. The division included Fender Guitar, Rhodes Piano, and Rogers Drums. Unbeknownst to Aunt Connie, they had tried to recruit Uncle Bob for months. They moved to Tustin, California, where a couple of years later Dan, with invitation, would arrive summer 1974 to work and live, reconnecting with our old friends after years of separation.

After October 1974, our families remained primarily separated by geography but also by our individual struggles regarding Dan's death. Bob Bull and our father remained close friends, but shared a wound that never healed before our father's death nine years after his oldest son's.

Daniel My Brother

One of the newspapers reporting Dan's murder described him as a "rootless young man." That never sat well with me. Dan had great home roots. He had solid guidance and support from two sets of parents. Into his late teens and early twenties, Dan, motivated by an inherent drive for adventure mixed with conflict at home (not uncommon for the times) was simply more interested in travel than planting roots. Also, how many people have their own roots deeply planted at twenty-one?

The truth is, Dan was a completely normal kid, teenager, and young adult. He was above average as a risk-taker, trading caution for experiences. Dan's extensive travel may have separated him from the crowd, but he was a regular guy. The only thing about Dan's life that was truly abnormal was how it ended.

I was considerably younger than my two siblings and, as such, a "pain in the butt" as a younger brother. One evening as kids, Dan and I sat on the couch watching TV. Dan was playing with matches. He struck one and, for a joke, touched it to my sock. POOF! My first combustive experience. I was both fascinated and in shock. Before it could spread—in fact, before I could blink—Dan threw his body on my foot to snuff out the flames like a soldier diving on a live grenade to save his comrades. He swore me to silence so forcefully it sank in. This is the first time I've broken that confidence.

Dan was in and out of my life going to college, traveling, and "finding himself" as I entered my teens, which was OK with me. It was cool watching him during those years of travel and rebellion. During a Pony League baseball game, a teammate got my attention and said, "Hey, take a look at the nice-looking girl behind home plate, behind the fence." I got up from the corner of the dugout to look and spotted Dan who had shown up to catch a couple innings of our game. It thrilled me to see my brother, and I responded to my teammate, "Yeah, she really is beautiful. That's my brother with her."

Dan was a traveler, a seeker of independence, not looking for a cookie-cutter life. He was aiming for a life less ordinary, whatever it might be. The universe didn't design him to wear polished wingtips or loafers to work like his father. He was a voracious reader, devouring classic works by many authors. School assignments began the practice, but it became a habit. He retained passages important to him and often quoted them in letters to friends and family.

There was an intensity to Dan that combined with the turbulent crazy years in which he lived—well, it makes a story. In my view, he was one of those people who put principle over profit. His entry into the carpentry profession at the time of his death was as much a statement, part of his rebellion, as it was a means of making a living and pursuing his dream of building his own boat and sailing the world. Would he have stayed that way? Who knows? Many idealists loosen those tightly held ideals when reality hits them squarely in the bank account. Life will do that.

Dan was, as they say, "wise beyond his years," in my opinion. I dislike clichés, that one in particular, but I had heard Debbie (and others) say it more than once. And she was the older, often—judgmental sister, and Dan's harshest critic.

By no means could I claim to be a student of literature. I have only scratched the surface of what scholars consider canonized writing. However, I was struck by a passage in *The Count of Monte Cristo* comparing "learners" to the "learned"—Memory making the learners, philosophy the learned. I'm sure I love that excerpt purely because of Dan.

Even at his young age, Dan was well on his way to being one of the learned. I say so partly because of the gifts he gave me.

The first was a popular book by a French author for my birthday. It bore an inscription from Dan that became more meaningful to me than the book itself.

At that age, I didn't clearly understand the message he was attempting to send his younger brother in this best-selling novella. In fact, I couldn't bring myself to read it until long after Dan's death.

In our many moves over the years, that book left our custody, possibly inadvertently, in a garage sale. God, I wish I could get **that** book back, that copy of *The Little Prince*. I wish I had Dan's inscription on the back of the front cover. I remember it started out:

Doug,

There comes a time in a person's life when they dig for knowledge. A deeper knowledge than 2+2=4 or the capital of _____ is _____.

It went on, but that's all I remember.

The next gift I received from Dan was a simple read about self-determination, breaking away from the norm, blazing one's own path, and seeking independence despite what others think. The inscription inside the cover of *Jonathan Livingston Seagull* reads in part:

Doug,

Limitations, there really are none. Only the ones we put on ourselves.

Oh, how right you were, Dan. How right you were. Thanks!

Dan was home in between his travels. I think he was nineteen or twenty and I was still an early teen when he came into my room in the mid-afternoon and asked, "Can I read to you?"

As a young teenager whose main interests were football, baseball, and hockey, my first reaction was, *This is weird*, but I said yes. At first, I was uncomfortable, but my brother was just trying to connect, and connect he did. He was building his relationship with me, giving me his time, making me matter in his life.

He was also trying to influence me, which he did more than he will ever know. I remember my discomfort fading and enjoying having my older brother spend time with me. I remember a gentleness about him.

That calmness, that gentleness, is highlighted in a favorite story of the Bull girls, Martha, Leslie, and Julie. I think all three of them have repeated this story to me more than once over the years.

Everyone loves nicer cars, but they weren't a luxury the Bulls or our family indulged in. Quite the opposite. Upscale expensive cars were never a thing in our lives growing up. Uncle Bob's new 1967 MGB and Danny and Deb's $600 used MGB might have been the most extravagant vehicles ever owned between our two families.

I don't know which older, modestly priced automobile the Bulls owned when Dan was visiting during the summer 1974, but on the way to the beach one day, the car broke down on the L.A. Freeway. David, Dan, and the three girls were stranded on the shoulder. Their hopes of having a fun day at the beach vanished as they waited for a wrecker to retrieve them from the busy highway. The girls were upset and remember David getting demonstrably angry that this disastrous turn had disrupted their day. Dan on the other hand spread his beach towel on the top of the car and kicked back to catch some rays, urging the group to make the best of a bad hop. Dan was living in the now, not worrying about things he couldn't do anything about. Travel, life, involves unexpected twists, turns, and disruptions beyond one's control. By that time, Dan had traveled enough to know the adventure lies not in the destination but the journey.

The Trip to Abilene and Buffalo Gap

I peered over my shoulder past my spouse and partner, Loretta, to the door of the restaurant. I drew an anxious breath and grabbed another sip off my Coors tallboy. Being just past eleven in the morning, it was way too early for beer, but I rationalized that if it ever made sense to have one early, today was one of those days. It was just one for now to settle a couple of nerves. Probably wouldn't finish it anyway. I should have ordered a standard twelve-ounce, but Coors only came in tallboys at this Mexican restaurant, and I was in a nostalgic mood, remembering a time when you could only get Coors in the Midwest if you smuggled it in from the Mountain West. My only worry was having beer breath while meeting someone new face-to-face for the first time. Loretta had chewing gum at the ready to help cover my morning beer breath. She was nursing a club soda, always the more prudent one, always with gum.

The previous evening, October 1, 2010, we had flown into Dallas/Fort Worth from Minneapolis/Saint Paul. We rented a car from Alamo, a silver Nissan Altima, and headed west toward Abilene, about a two-and-a-half-hour drive. We got a room at the Hampton Inn in Abilene and spent the evening reviewing our notes and questions.

It had been an interesting year. Like a favorite song or treasured film, it had created tension, stirred emotion, and now was building toward its crescendo. This afternoon, following a year of research, would be the most intense of the last twelve months.

In 2009, I began to act on something that had been gnawing at me for decades. Periodic nudges from Loretta over the last twelve years also helped me start the journey. To varying degrees, further motivation came from fielding inquiries from my sister's three daughters about my brother, their uncle, a man none of them had known.

My oldest niece is Dan's godchild, who was six months old when he was killed. She posed the fewest questions over the years. However, for a school research project, she asked how I felt about the death penalty after what happened to Dan. Later, as my sister's middle and youngest daughters came into their rebellious years and their mother started comparing them to Dan, they came to me for further information.

During one of those conversations, one of my nieces asked if I still had any possessions of Dan's. I thought for a moment, then led her to our garage where there was still a part of Dan's old wooden toolbox. It was a socket storage tray from a toolbox he had crafted himself while living in California and working for a sailboat manufacturer as a carpenter. The toolbox itself had fallen apart many years earlier, a victim of neglect, but time was bound to take its toll on such an item. I picked up the socket tray and handed it to my niece, who, as she held it, shed tears for a man gone years before her birth. It just happened to be October 1.

Each niece since the mid-nineties had come to me periodically seeking more details regarding my brother. All three came to me for the same reason. Their mother, my sister, simply didn't want to talk about it with them.

Every so often, over a couple of glasses of wine, my sister's emotions regarding Dan would surface. Those vulnerable tipsy moments, however, were only that—emotion. She never yielded the details her daughters sought, and once the wine wore off, so did any urge to reminisce about Dan.

My sister's feelings regarding Dan were complicated, and I've never questioned them. The two were closer in age, and her relationship with him was wholly different from mine. She and Dan were best friends at times and each other's harshest critics at others. They had spent almost two years together at the same university, St. Norbert in De Pere, Wisconsin, just a few miles from Green Bay.

Debbie was in her final stretch of college seeking a teaching degree. Dan was in his second year, philosophizing, partying, flirting, experimenting, and protesting the war in Vietnam. They were brother and sister but very different. Debbie was the quintessential responsible oldest child dutifully fulfilling parental expectations. Dan was the second child determined to take a different path. Rebellious, one could say, but that wouldn't be unusual given the time in American history. Despite Debbie and Dan's differences, their brotherly and sisterly love was strong, and they were each other's confidants whenever home life seemed crazy. I wasn't part of their bond. I was too young. I've respected her boundaries regarding Dan and have rarely breached the subject.

My sister's resistance on the subject was broader than, "I don't care to talk about it." That wasn't really it. She just wasn't going to volunteer anything. The question from my sister to her three girls was probably and legitimately, "What do you want to know?" But her kids didn't know the questions to ask. Furthermore, in my sister's defense, where does one begin? It's very much a had-to-be-there story. You had to know Dan for any of it to make sense. Or in a way, less sense. You had to know the times.

It sounds so callous the way my sister sometimes treated the subject, an attitude that in no way reflected a lack of love for her brother. Rather, it was a defense mechanism. Her mantra when times were rough was, "*Get over it!*" A strong front protecting a fragile interior, a strategic deflection born of Dan's incident.

My sister is a tough and resilient woman. She is a positive-attitude survivor of multiple traumas, not the least of which was a severe chainsaw accident. The blade sank into her left thigh to her femur.

Among many other oldest child responsibilities over the years, Debbie also had the unenviable task of being my father's wing person in mid-October 1974, in San Bernardino, California, a task unsuited for our mother, anyone's mother, at any time. A two-day whirlwind trip, accompanied by Bob Bull, to deal with Dan's Volkswagen bus and go through his belongings, deciding what to keep and what not to keep. Some items were being held as evidence.

Debbie was an adventurous soul and curious about this world as anyone. All three of us kids had that trait, perhaps in some degree inherited from our father. Or maybe Debbie and I were further inspired by Dan. I don't know from whence our adventure and travel bug originated, but both Debbie and I caught it.

There were a couple of Griswold-style-family road trips growing up. Not as nutty but crazy enough. When we could afford it, we went on road trips to see relatives in Louisiana. Such trips were always out of the ordinary. Debbie and I both loved taking road trips. Nurture or nature, it's in us. The lengthier, and more challenging and tiring, the better.

Surprising to me—shocking I might say—my sister, at forty-two, having never been on a motorcycle in her life, invited herself on a ten-day bike trip through the Rocky Mountains I had planned in 1992. I was happy to have her along. She was a patient, enthusiastic, fun-loving traveling companion.

I advised her against joining me across the Great Plains on a bike, so she flew to Bozeman, Montana, rented a car, and toured Yellowstone for two days by herself. We met in Jackson, Wyoming. I followed her to the airport to return her car. It was the same day President George H. W. Bush was campaigning in Jackson, where he had just delivered a speech at the airport. As we drove north from town on Highway 191, we caught a glimpse of Air Force One taking off with the Tetons in the background.

After returning her car, my 5'0" tall sister emerged from the airport car rental office, smiled at me, and asked, "OK, how do I get on?" That was when I realized she had never been on a motorcycle before, ever, in her life. We spent a memorable ten days zigzagging through the Rockies until she flew back to Wisconsin from Albuquerque, New Mexico, once again, avoiding the monotonous Great Plains. The way I marathoned my way back to Minnesota from Albuquerque on my Virago 1100, in the pouring rain at times, would've scared her to death. Honestly, it scared me, but I've always relied on a guardian spirit to guide me through my more difficult and sometimes dangerous adventures.

Even though my sister was an eager and fearless traveler, if her itinerary took her on Interstate 40 in California, between Needles and Barstow, she rerouted to avoid that stretch of road.

I, too, had packed away Dan's incident. However, the aligning of events surrounding his death had intrigued me from the beginning. I was more than happy to be my niece's information conduit on the subject. I wanted them to know who their uncle was. I thought it was important. If I didn't give them information and if my sister wasn't a willing source, how would they ever find out about their long-lost uncle? But I didn't know enough, or I had forgotten.

The story the way I knew it, from everything I had seen, heard, and read over the years, had incredible twists. I'd always thought I should tell it, but I never made the time or summoned the emotional energy to take on the task. Debbie was never going to embark on such a quest.

Perhaps enough time had passed to overcome the resistance. We were getting older, and the story risked going untold. I was the only one who could tell it. Loretta and I finally, after much soul-searching, took our first tentative steps toward what we called "The Project."

Scant remnants of Dan remained in my possession in the backs of drawers or other nooks around the house. One was a tattered, faded, three-by-five-inch index card with six ink-smeared names and phone numbers, friends from St. Norbert, I presumed. It was folded in a way that it likely had come from Dan's wallet. I had saved it in my desk drawer all those years for reasons unknown.

I knew my sister had a plastic bin of family memorabilia in her basement, which fortunately had mostly survived a washing machine malfunction flood. Loretta and I asked for that bin on our next visit back to Baraboo, Wisconsin, over Thanksgiving, 2009.

Our walk back in time had begun.

Digging Through Memories

I had always hoped my older brother's story could be told somehow, someway, but like everyone else affected, I had long ago put it out of my mind and had moved on. I had a career, as did Loretta. Our lives were peaceful. Telling the story would take a fair amount of research, which would take time and emotional investment. By 2009, feeling secure in my career, I could make time for a side project, and by then, maybe the emotional parts wouldn't be as thorny as they once were.

Loretta and I dug through the bin and scanned old family photos and handwritten letters. Deeper were the police reports, the investigation follow-up communications, and newspaper clippings—memorabilia I remember being stored in a shoebox in the bottom of my parents closet in Libertyville in the late-seventies. We scanned it all for later reference.

Loretta and I thoroughly reviewed the information and discussed our next steps. Talk to folks who knew Dan, an obvious initial action. Reviewing information I hadn't seen in years brought forth a question filed in the back of my mind, one that had nagged at me since I was fifteen. Now I had another voicing that same curiosity.

"Wouldn't it be interesting to find out who the hitchhiker was? And talk to him?" A wistful thought but nothing else in my mind.

Armed with a cheap recorder from Loretta's college years and a haphazard list of questions, we took a weekend jaunt to the Chicago area in early spring 2010 to conduct some interviews. First on our list were three of our lifelong friends: David Bull, Martha Bull Nadeau, and Leslie Bull.

David's relationship with Dan was different from that of Dan's neighborhood crew and schoolmates. They were very close in age. Less than five months separated them, but Dan was a grade ahead. The two boys were more like brothers because of the close-knit nature of our families. Their personalities complimented each other, as did their fathers. David and Dan, when they were in their early twenties, were hatching grand traveling schemes together. David's first child, a boy, was born in 1986. He named him Danny.

Growing up, the two older Bull girls always looked up to and wanted to hang with their brother and Dan, especially Martha, who was closest in age and interests. The older boys were the cool kids, the leaders of the Bull-Walker pack.

The youngest of the four Bull children was the friend I had known the longest in my life. Julie was three months my junior, born on the Fourth of July, and determined to prove it. Julie and I, being the youngest of the two families and so close in age, were accomplices in spoiled-kid escapades growing up. After about 1969, the two of us got together less frequently, but to this day, I never lost my love for her. I can almost recite from memory the letter she wrote me at fifteen October 2, 1974, at 1 a.m.

Because of how close Julie and I were, whenever we got together over the years, no subject was off limits, including Dan. She expressed her emotions and gave me her view of that summer in 1974 numerous times. We discovered through these discussions that we both had the same recurring dream for a long time after that fateful October day. Dan wasn't gone. It was all a ruse. It was someone's bad joke, maybe Dan's.

The most poignant and emotional exchange of information between us occurred one night in late June 1977 in California. It was the first time

I had seen her and her family in six or seven years and the first time seeing her since Dan's death. We had slipped away from Julie's family and my sunburned traveling companion and were visiting a friend of Julie's where, with substantial help, we didn't sleep. For twelve hours, no one interrupted our conversation about Dan and that summer of '74. We drove back to the Bull's Santa Ana home the following morning in David's VW van as the sun rose with Led Zeppelin's *Physical Graffiti* cranked on the eight track. It was a memorable night with my oldest friend.

The Bull kids were the closest to this story, so getting their impressions of that time was the next logical step. I was hesitant to ask our friends to revisit a time in their lives that they likely would rather not think about. We strived to talk mostly about the plentiful good times our families had shared, but the events of early October 1974 hung like an approaching dark cloud over each conversation.

Since their migrations back to Illinois, the Bulls, my sister, and I sometimes spoke about Dan but never in any detail or depth and certainly never on tape. There was no need to rehash the past. We had a front seat to a story we knew all too well. Or so we thought. Turns out everyone had only fragmented knowledge of what had happened. Those who loved Dan the most sometimes knew the least. Everyone had run from the pain immediately, putting up a stiff arm to additional information.

We hit the Chicago area early Saturday afternoon. Leslie Bull was our first interview. Perhaps the clearest headed of the seven Bull and Walker kids because she didn't engage in the partying shenanigans the rest of us did. Leslie was caught between not being included with the older kids and not wanting to hang with us younger kids. Leslie was more interested in her studies and almost always had her "nose to the grindstone" in such endeavors. A soft-spoken woman. She reaffirmed her great fondness for our parents, highlighting how fun and laidback she thought they were. When the conversation turned to Dan, the tears flowed immediately. Leslie loved Dan like another brother. Leslie was an undergrad freshman at Pepperdine in her dorm room on October 1, 1974, living by herself when she got the bad news.

David was, as he jokingly put it, our next victim that afternoon. As a former Military Intelligence NCO, five years active, twenty in reserve, one could understand his discomfort, but he consented to be interviewed and recorded. According to others in his immediate family, David stored the more difficult of these memories in a secure and private place. However, he made an exception for us this time and went as deep as he ever had on the subject.

David spoke of his love and respect for our parents and the good times spent at the Walker house on Diamond Lake growing up. He learned to water ski on that lake with Uncle Dan piloting the boat and Danny spotting and cheering him on. He told us stories of Dan's time visiting them the summers of 1968 and 1969 in Utah at The Homestead Resort. He filled in detail about Dan's time staying with them the summer of 1974 and their trip to Mexico the weekend before Dan left and was murdered. He told us where he was when he got the news and the utter chaos that overtook their world in the immediate aftermath. He called Dan his best friend and said he'd been unable to call someone that ever again.

"At least the nightmares went away a while ago," he confessed.

Martha was our final interview that Saturday. It went long into the evening. Drinks were involved and tears flowed the moment we began. She and Dan had gotten close late the summer of 1974. David, Dan, and Martha had celebrated Martha's nineteenth birthday in Mexico, partying in cantinas and camping on a Pacific Ocean beach south of Ensenada. After the memorable weekend, Dan had invited Martha to hit the road with him, but she had declined, saying, "Danny, I can't just run off with you." What would have happened if she had? Would Dan have taken the same route? Would he have picked up a hitchhiker? Would Martha have helped drive through the night instead of stopping to rest? Would she have lost her life along with Dan? Would she have been a witness instead of the hitchhiker?

Before the six-hour drive back to Minnesota Sunday afternoon, we interviewed two other folks in that northeast Illinois area. Rick Corrado was one of Dan's college roommates at St. Norbert, and one of the names on the three-by-five index card from Dan's wallet. He generously gave us some time despite having never met us. He described his time at St. Norbert with Dan as "right out of a movie." Rick left St. Norbert, transferring to De Paul University the same time Dan dropped out of school for good. Things had gotten too intense up in De Pere that winter and spring of 1972.

Our final connection that weekend was with one of our neighbors growing up, Kevin O'Donnell. The O'Donnells were a solidly Irish Catholic family of seven kids who attended the same schools and lived down the street. Kevin was an interesting, creative person. He was a professional songwriter/musician, artist, photographer, beekeeper, and author—side jobs to his engineering and consulting career. Kevin had recently published a book about his family's migration from Ireland, titled *Fado': A Memoir of Life Liberty and the Pursuit of Happiness*. Kevin's oldest brother, John O'Donnell (aka Jay), now deceased, was Dan's first friend in Mundelein. On his eighteenth birthday, in a letter to his friend Michelle, Dan wrote about meeting John and reminiscing about life in the "good old" days.

October 15, 1970

Then there was my first friend when we moved to Mundelein. I was sitting on a slab of cement across from this crewcut kid. We were all in good sport shirts and dark blue pants and a blue bow tie.

"Hi!" the crewcut kid said. He was tall and lanky (compared to me). He had green eyes with long eyelashes and dark eyebrows.

"Hi!" I said, feeling a red flush come over my face. "Are you new here?" he asked bashfully. "Yep." I felt more at ease now.

We talked of frogs and tadpoles and mothers and what we each had for lunch. He ate his typical mayonnaise sandwich, an apple, and candy bar. I had my usual peanut butter without jelly, an apple, and candy bar. The bell rang and we were back in class.

Walking home I saw the same kid walking my way. I hadn't made any friends yet but I was eager to do so.

"Hey kid," I bellowed.

"Yes?"

"What's your name? Can I walk with ya?"

"John O'Donnell...yes!"

John (Jay) and my brother were in the same Cub Scouts den, attended the same private Catholic schools, and traveled parts of the world together before sharing a house with other buds in Denver in 1973 and the first half of 1974. John O'Donnell would be one of the first to be contacted by California law enforcement October 1, 1974, because of the Colorado registration on Dan's motorcycle in the back of the van. Police asked him if there would be any identifiable marks or jewelry to help confirm the victim's identity.

"The only thing I know of is the rope necklace around Dan's neck holding a wooden whistle," answered John.

As one would expect, it was an emotionally exhausting weekend, but it was also fruitful. We got more from our meetings than I ever thought we would. Everyone was interested in sharing memories and thoughts of Dan and the times.

There was another figure from Dan's life I had been curious to find for years. He also grew up with Dan and was another good friend. He, too, was one of the neighborhood guys, an import to the hood from Milwaukee when he was in eighth grade. Bob Schneider now lived in Sherman Oaks, California.

I had liked Bob. I was fond of all of Dan's friends growing up. I had always wondered where Bob had ended up and always wanted to talk with him again.

Almost immediately after connecting on social media, Bob and I had an extensive phone conversation. I learned he and his wife, Julie Henthorn, had named their third son Dan.

Bob was just finishing up a career as an executive with Warner Brother's Entertainment and had invested in a small business in Palm Desert, California. Bob and Julie had sold their Sherman Oaks home and would be moving in a few months.

Bob was likely one of the more grounded members of the crew Dan had hung with back in the sixties and early-seventies—Carmel High School for Boys class secretary and a good student. Bob enrolled at De Paul after high school, got his degree, and became lifelong friends with Dan's old roommate Rick Corrado. During those years, Bob didn't participate too heavily in some of the riskier activities of his closer friends.

We caught Bob and Julie at a good time. They invited us to stay at their place for a couple of nights during our trip to California, a trip that was already in its planning stages.

Around the same time, I had contacted the San Bernardino County, California, sheriff's department's cold case team and was in the process of setting up an appointment with a detective named Greg Myler to discuss Dan's case.

Also planned for our California trip was an attempt to replicate Dan's last drive. We thought it might be interesting to retrace the route Dan likely took out of Southern California the evening of September 30, 1974. Our cold case meeting would be along the way.

Attempting to be an efficient traveler and use my vacation time wisely, I had combined our California research trip with a required weekend business conference in Scottsdale, Arizona. We planned to do our five-plus days of discovery in Southern California, drop off Loretta at Sky Harbor in Phoenix on Friday morning, and attend the conference. I would cap off the trip with a Sunday drive back west through Joshua Tree National Park and take in a Dodgers game that Sunday afternoon. I would fly home from LAX on Monday morning.

So, it was the first week of August 2010 that we headed off to Southern California for the next stage of our journey. The first night was a cordial visit with my brother-in-law's sister and old friend of mine, Bridget Terry, a graduate of Northwestern University and longtime veteran of the Southern California entertainment industry. She had known Dan but only briefly. They had partied together a couple of times at family events. Bridget was a bridesmaid and Dan was a groomsman in Debbie's marriage to her brother Denis on September 30, 1972. Having never received any information from those in the know, Bridget thought Dan had been stabbed to death.

The next two nights, Bob Schneider and his wife, Julie Henthorn, graciously hosted us at their quintessential California Hills home. Our visit with Bob was everything I had hoped it would be—comfortable, honest, and informative.

Almost everything Bob shared about his Mundelein days and friendship with Dan was poignant. He told us stories and added context about Dan that we would've never otherwise known. The crazy stuff they all did as late teens. The time Dan scared him to death doing 100 MPH in Bob's girlfriend's Jensen Healey. He filled us in on other Mundelein and post-high-school friends of Dan's. He described his peer group's experience and views of the Vietnam War and what he knew of Dan's time in college and subsequent exit from college. He recounted crazy times in Denver when Bob visited, the phone conversation he had with Dan as he was deciding to leave California and, of course, Dan's death and the aftermath for him and Dan's other friends.

One shared moment between Bob and me occurred during a run to the liquor store. Standing in front of the beer cooler, he said, "You know, your dad was pretty strict."

I could see how he saw it that way. We'd also found out that Bob had been present at some critical, often turbulent, exchanges between my father and brother. I didn't want to disagree with Bob. I just nodded and said, "Things changed quite a bit after Dan." Things did change, not surprisingly so, but "strict" wasn't quite the word I'd use to describe my father in those days.

After leaving Bob and Julie's, we headed to the Bull's old Lemona Lane address in Tustin to start the retracing of Dan's last drive. From Lemona Lane we worked our way toward Interstate 15—old Route 66—then up toward Cajon Pass where the police report said Dan had picked up his hitchhiker. Our retracing would take us through Victorville, Barstow, then east toward Needles. But first our critical stop was in San Bernardino.

We got a hotel about a mile south of the sheriff's office and started our fourth day with a morning meeting with Detective Greg Myler, a professional above professionals, in my view, who handled only cold cases. He was smartly dressed in a pressed striped shirt and tie and couldn't have made himself more available to us. He gave us as much time as we needed and answered as many of our questions as he could. It was a unique experience, but if we had expected any new revelations that might help solve this decades old case (which personally I hadn't), they were dashed. The case remained as it was in late 1974 into 1975.

Ice cold.

Greg had a file about eight inches thick in front of him. I asked, "You're not going to give me any access to that file are you?"

"You really don't want to see some of the things that are in here," he said, "and there are details we can track back to the perpetrators. I can't compromise the case by giving you access to the file."

After more than thirty-five years of no progress, I couldn't see how we could possibly compromise anything, but then I wasn't completely sure I wanted to see what was in the file anyway. I didn't press the issue.

Early into our hour-long meeting that yielded little new information about the case, I asked if I could try one important nagging question. He predicted it.

"What was the hitchhiker's name?"

"Yeah." I laughed.

"Ken Robinson is his name. It's on the first page of the case summary, the brief I printed for your visit," Greg replied.

Loretta and I both had a copy of that brief sitting in front of us, but with our early attention focused on Greg and our list of questions, we hadn't glanced at it yet, presuming it was just an overview of information we already knew. It mostly was, except for the last few words in the first paragraph. "Inside the vehicle with Daniel is a hitchhiker named Kenneth Glenn Robinson."

Loretta and I looked at each other with shock. Really, it was that easy? Then I blurted, "Are you kidding me? All we had to do was ask?"

We had learned more than we expected researching our project, but if there was one thing we were more curious about than anything else. It truly was the hitchhikers's identity. Now, after thirty-six years, we had a name to go with the moniker.

"Would you like me to see if I can get hold of him? Would you want to speak with him?" Detective Myler asked.

The question caught me momentarily off guard, but I answered, "Yes! Absolutely!"

My mind, though, was in a different place. Articles and police reports said the man was from Texas, but it seemed unlikely after all these years that we could find him. Isn't that the nature of hitchhikers? They don't have wheels. A bed is where they can find it, calling no place particular home. They are in your car briefly then just a figure in your rearview mirror, vanishing forever, just like the killers, just like Dan. In that moment, I dismissed the possibility.

We thanked Detective Myler for his time and resumed our tracing of Dan's route. We had the six-page-long case summary, including a map with relevant locations and times of the events that October morning. Loretta read the summary aloud while I drove. There really wasn't much new information in the summary. It revealed the name of the beer truck driver who had stopped to help the murderers get unstuck that morning. His name was Macias. The summary also disclosed the other party who had helped get the hitchhiker and Dan to the Needles hospital in their camper. And it highlighted the early-1975 efforts to find the Whittier, California, seller of the gold van the murderers claimed they had recently purchased.

Not that far from San Bernardino on Interstate 15 near Cajon Pass, we guessed the approximate place where Dan had picked up his hitchhiker, Ken Robinson. Wow! We had the man's name!

From there we hit all the places of significance along Interstate 15 and Interstate 40, including the restaurant where Dan and Ken had stopped for something to eat not long after Dan had picked him up. The Ludlow Cafe, where two witnesses, both waitresses, told the police the killers had something to eat at 2:30 a.m. (another of the few new pieces of information from Greg Myler in our summary). We guessed where Macias, the beer truck driver, helped the suspects at 5:30 a.m. west of Ludlow and, finally, the spot where the pair had crossed paths with Dan and his hitchhiker. Sixty-two miles west of Needles and about three miles east of Kelbaker Road, it looked like a place someone tired from driving might pull off. It felt like the right place, too. I think both of us felt it.

I had never been to this place before. Surprisingly, no one in our family had ever visited the spot in the last thirty-six years. Not that going there would have provided any revelation, comfort, or solace.

The place where Dan and his hitchhiker pulled off that morning was big enough to be called a parking lot. You could tell the California Highway Department was discouraging pulling off there by building graveled speed bumps in the area. There was a huge rise, a natural hill straight to the west blocking the view of eastbound traffic. To the south and southeast, a desert view with mountains in the background. For the desert, a pretty place. Desolate except for the interstate.

We walked the parking area, each in our own world. How is one to feel? We were there about ten minutes, interstate traffic whizzing by while I reflected and tried to imagine the scene that October 1 morning. As I walked to the car, I found what Loretta had been up to. She had cleared a place and arranged stones to form the initials DAW with a peace sign below. We climbed back into the car and continued toward Needles.

I was glad I came here. I should have done so earlier. I no longer had to imagine the scene, the place where Dan had died.

Our last stop for the research portion of the trip was the hospital in Needles, California, where Dan and the hitchhiker were taken that morning. It was more than an hour's ride. From what we knew, that must have been a horrific ride for this guy we now knew was named Ken Robinson.

There wasn't much to see. It was a small-town hospital. We took a picture of the emergency room door as we circled through the parking lot.

It had been a long, emotional day, few days. We decided to exit Interstate 40 and stay in Lake Havasu. Neither of us had been there before, and we wanted to check out the fabled London Bridge the night before Loretta flew out, and I would report for weekend work duty.

The Southern California part of our fact-finding tour was complete, and I was thrilled with the outcome of our research over the past ten months. We had connected with people from the past, folks I had dearly wanted to catch up with for years. We had fun conversations about Dan and gathered some fresh information. The research had been gratifying and interesting, perhaps cathartic. However, the research hadn't yet yielded enough additional information to persuade me to move our little project further.

I had dropped off Loretta at Sky Harbor airport around noon the next day and checked into the Scottsdale resort. I was getting ready for the weekend business conference and catching up on emails I had ignored all week. That's when my cell phone rang.

The Connection

It was from an unfamiliar area code. I considered letting it roll to voicemail. We had roommates at this corporate meeting, so I had walked onto the balcony of the hotel room to take the call.

I hit the answer button on my Blackberry and recited my normal business greeting. "Hello. This is Doug, how can I help you?"

"Mr. Walker. This is Kenneth Robinson."

"Oh my God!" I gasped into the phone.

"Hi."

I didn't know what to say. My mind raced. I had just heard his name for the first time two days ago and now I was on the phone with him.

"I've been wantin' to talk with you for thirty-six years," Kenneth Robinson said. "You have no idea how much this means to me. In my life, your brother is a hero. I believe he saved my life."

The man on the other end was crying, and shivers took hold of my body.

Of all times to have less than optimal cell phone coverage! I wanted to talk to this man. I desperately wanted to continue this call. As important as this phone call was to me, we needed to be able to hear each other. Every word, clearly.

I begged understanding from Ken.

"Ken, for some reason, my cell signal isn't that good. I'm only catching part of what you are saying, and I need to hear everything. Plus, I need to be in a business meeting in about ten minutes. Can I call you back when I get better reception and corporate America isn't demanding my time?"

I felt sick. It felt awful trying to end the call. Ken reluctantly agreed. He told me to call anytime I broke free, and we both hung up.

I was shaken. My heart pounded as I returned to the room from the balcony.

My roommate was also from the Minneapolis area but brand new with the company. I barely knew him. He could probably see the shocked and dazed look on my face as I reentered the room. It was too long and too personal a story to relate, especially to someone I didn't know well.

This was unbelievably bad timing. I may have been waiting for this call or conversation in the back of my mind for the last thirty-six years, but I had other commitments. I slipped my notebook from my briefcase and started toward the weekend's kickoff meeting with my roommate. My phone rang again as the door to our room shut behind us from another unfamiliar number. Given all that was going on, I answered it.

"Hello. This is Doug, how can I help you?" I answered again, hustling down the hallway to the elevator.

"Doug, this is Greg Myler. Did you get a phone call?"

Overwhelmed again, I responded.

"Yes, I did! Just now! I just this moment hung up."

For some reason, Greg Myler was coming through crystal clear.

"Man, that was quick. He strongly expressed his desire to talk to you," Greg said. "He really wanted to talk with me! I think he wants to share anything and everything with anyone who will listen."

I still had to be in a meeting in just a few minutes, so I thanked Greg for all his help and hung up. Moments later, I walked into our company's Friday evening kickoff meeting of 700 or so corporate associates. My head was in a very different place.

I called Ken back during a break the next morning from a part of the resort that was under renovation. No one was around, not even the construction crew. Ken and I were still emotional, but at least we had a better signal. I promised to send information to him. I was still in and out of meetings until Sunday morning, so we agreed I would fly to Texas to visit as soon as possible. We needed to see each other and talk face-to-face. Anything further needed to be shared in person. He needed it and I needed it. Dan deserved it.

Before we hung up, Ken asked me a question.

"Do you want to know what your brother's last words to me were?"

Other than what the newspapers and police reported, I had never considered what Dan's last words might have been. What they reported could only have come from Ken himself. It had never occurred to me to think anything other than what I already knew. But clearly it was something Ken had never forgotten.

"Yes, I do," I responded.

Ken choked up and replied, "I'm just going to sit up here and catch the sunrise."

There was silence on the phone for a few moments.

"Those were Dan's last words to me before I climbed into the back of the van to sleep."

My eyes welled up. It sounded like something Dan would say. Tears had flowed quite often over the last eleven months of research, but those initial calls with Ken had brought about the heaviest emotion. I guess the emotional parts had remained thorny. I suspected new information was making them thornier.

Ken and I spoke a couple of times after our initial phone conversations in Phoenix. I sent scanned copies of letters, news articles, and police reports. He wanted pictures of Dan, and I sent them. He emailed me the next day that he was overwhelmed seeing photos of Dan. He admitted weeping over the images.

Loretta and I immediately planned a trip to see Ken. It made sense that it was around October 1.

A Long-Overdue Meeting

I peeked at the front door of the restaurant again, no action at all. We had gotten to Abuelo's right when they opened at eleven. It was still a bit early for the lunch crowd. I took another small sip off the tallboy.

"Just thinking out loud," I said to Loretta. "I obviously don't know how this is going to go today. If everything goes well and we are back in Dallas by tonight or early tomorrow morning, what do you say we catch the Book Depository and the Grassy Knoll? I've never been there. Our flight doesn't leave until the late afternoon. I'll bet downtown Dallas will be quiet on a Sunday morning."

Loretta responded, "Let's stick to today's priorities. If it works, great. If not, well, next time."

I nodded, rubbing the sweat off the can of beer with my thumb.

"You nervous?" Loretta asked.

"Yes, absolutely! No, not really. God! I don't know! It feels right and long overdue to be here."

My eyes caught the opening door in the restaurant alcove. I watched a father and his young daughter enter and get seated by the host. My attention moved back to Loretta.

"I can't believe the quickness of these events after all this time, and all we ever had to do was ask. I wish I'd known that earlier."

Abuelo's was a nicely laid-out Mexican restaurant, part of a mall complex. They had lots of nice greenery in the restaurant part, and it looked like they served tasty food. The bar, separate from the dining area, was comfortable with marble tabletops.

Through the window, Loretta caught sight of a man approaching the restaurant and nudged my forearm.

"That could be him. He looks the right age," she said, throwing her chin in the man's direction.

Looking over, I nodded.

"Could I get a stick of gum? I'll go check," I said.

I popped in the gum and got up from the bar. Hoping the spearmint was doing its job, I walked toward the alcove and the front door of Abuelo's.

The man was about my height, broad shouldered with short brown hair and round face. He wore a button-down Oxford shirt, jeans, and boots. As he entered the restaurant, he caught me approaching with purpose. He seemed to know I was the person he was there to meet.

I approached and asked, "Are you Ken?"

The man answered in a low, West Texas drawl. "Yes, you must be Doug."

We extended our hands for a handshake that immediately became a heartfelt embrace.

Ken looked me over then asked the customary, "How was y'all's trip down?"

"Good. No airline or airport problems. We always seem to be lucky that way. I need some wood to knock on."

We laughed. Then Ken asked with some urgency, "I wouldn't feel good talkin' here. Do you mind if we take a ride? I'll drive!"

Loretta and I were on Ken's turf, so anywhere he wanted to talk, to share his story, was fine with us. I waved Loretta over and introduced her to Ken. Another spontaneous hug.

I conveyed Ken's wish to take a ride and talk in a place other than the restaurant and left the two briefly to throw some cash on the bar to cover the small tab and tip.

"Lead us to your wheels, sir!" I said upon my return, and the three of us walked to the parking lot.

"I'm over here in this red Nissan Frontier," Ken said. "It's a club cab. Real comfy!"

Loretta got into the back of the club cab and positioned herself in the middle so she could interact with both Ken and me. I climbed into the passenger seat.

Neither Loretta nor I had been to this part of Texas before. I had only heard of Abilene in old Westerns and wasn't sure if they were referring to Abilene, Texas, or Abilene, Kansas. Otherwise, never had given the town a second thought. Being with this man in West Central Texas was a place we should've visited long ago.

With everyone buckled in, Ken wound out of the mall parking lot and took a right.

"It's a straight shot to Buffalo Gap from here, and it's a real pretty drive," Ken said. "At least *I* think it is!"

"You were born in Buffalo Gap?"

"No," Ken answered. "We moved there when I was about ten. Most of my memories are in this area. The good, bad, some ugly, and everything in between."

As we slowed behind traffic for a stoplight, Loretta broke in.

"Ken, as Doug has probably mentioned, we have been on this journey for a number of months. We've spoken to quite a few people over that time. We have laughed and also shed some tears, but we don't want to miss a thing. We have recorded everything except our meeting with Greg Myler, for obvious reasons. Do you mind if we record our conversation?"

Ken stiffened. He looked at us but mostly at me then asked, "What do you plan on doing with this information, with these interviews?"

I thought for a moment on how to respond. Nothing may come from this project. I didn't want to set any expectations.

"Long before now, Ken, in fact, since I was fifteen, I thought Dan's story would be a compelling story to document. Meeting you has only made it that much more interesting, but honestly, what are we going to do with these recordings? I don't know. I'm not a writer. I don't know anyone interested in helping to write a story. I don't know what will come of all this information and these interviews. Maybe a published story, maybe nothing."

Ken sat silent for a few moments, staring straight ahead. We were still stuck behind traffic at the light.

"OK, if this does become something, even a news story, if anyone outside of us three gets access to our conversation, well, I want to review any information that may become public and maybe remove parts of what we talk about, and my name. Those killers are still out there. I don't want my name published or talked about without my consent."

That set me back on my heels. I had given up on us finding the killers a long time ago, much less them trying to find us. Ken was a witness, I knew, but after thirty-six years it seemed like an unwarranted fear.

"Another thing. I don't know, I've really wrestled with it," Ken said. "I don't know if I should tell y'all or not about Dan and me that night. If I was lookin' down at someone talkin' about me... Maybe there are things

I shouldn't talk 'bout with y'all. Not wantin' it repeated. It's nothin' bad, my gosh! Nothin' bad. Some might think so, but it's not the end of the world. You want to stop for a Coke or somethin' for the ride?"

Ken seemed uncomfortable and tentative. Understandably, I was too. This was all a little weird.

"We're good, I think," I answered, confirming with a look to Loretta over my shoulder. Why don't we keep driving and perhaps later we can go back to Abuelo's for a late lunch or early dinner? It looked like they have good food."

"That sounds good," said Ken. "I'll give you a tour of Buffalo Gap and then we'll go back and eat at Abuelo's later."

"Ken, no one will have access to what will be on the tapes, and nothing will be published without your prior consent and approval. I promise." There was a brief silence, another taking of a breath, a mutual assessment. I said, "Based on what we have shared over the phone and email, I believe this is as much your story as ours. Without you, nothing significant is really known, therefore, nothing is told."

Ken didn't know us, but he nodded to Loretta. He seemed ready to trust that we would keep our word. The light turned green, and traffic started moving. Loretta hit the record button.

"When that San Bernardino officer, Greg Myler called, I wasn't home," Ken began. "He somehow found the phone number of my daughter-in-law. She calls me and caught me in my truck on my way home from work. I put her on speaker, and man, I could hear it! She was so upset wondering what was goin' on! She and I love each other. We are as close as my own kids. She says, 'Papa? There's a detective in California trying to get a hold of ya.'"

Ken paused for a few seconds. He seemed to be gathering himself.

"Man, I'm tellin' ya, I was taken aback. I probably shouldn't have answered that call in my truck." Ken shook his head.

"My daughter-in-law knows zero about this. No one in my world really does, especially to any level of detail. It was, and still is, an unintentional secret. So I say, 'I know what this is about, I know what they're callin' about. There's nothin' to be concerned about,' is what I said to her but I'm sure I wasn't very convincing. After all this time, all these years, I don't think I was able to hide my reaction, even over the phone. I think she could hear the emotion in my voice. There really was nothin' for her to be worried about but the memories immediately came flooding back.

"She asks me, 'I have the detective's number. Do you want it?' I said, 'Yes! I want that number, and I want it right now!' I pulled to the side of the road to write it down."

The way Ken emphasized his eagerness for Greg Myler's number and the time I knew it took for him to call me caused a chill to pass through my body. Putting myself in Ken's shoes, getting that phone call after all those years, had to have been a jolt.

"Obviously, I had no idea why they were callin'. My first thought was they caught 'em, and they need me to identify 'em. I called that detective up, Greg Myler, right there from the side of the road. He's in cold cases in San Bernardino, right?"

"Yes," I confirmed.

"Fortunately, I haven't had to interact with many cops over the years, so I don't have a large sample size, but Officer Myler seemed like a true professional. I was extremely impressed with the man."

Ken nodded.

"My son is a cop in Abilene. I obviously have a great respect for people in that line of work. Anyway, I tell Greg, 'There's so many regrets I have, but the one thing that has eaten at me the most is I've had no one to talk to about what happened. No person, no reason, no nothin'. I've had no one to talk to 'bout Dan. Then Greg goes, 'I'm glad you said that because he's got a brother who really wants to talk to you.' I cried like a baby when I heard those words. I had been racing to this moment my whole life, even if I didn't know it. I said, 'Please give me his number.'"

The chills persisted. A tear tried to burst out. I resisted, barely.

"Anyway, I didn't call you immediately, but, uh, I worked up enough courage to."

Loretta jumped in.

"It was pretty quick, Ken. We were pretty shocked watching and feeling the chain of events unfold as quickly as they did once we got your name. For how many years, we wondered?"

Ken smiled at Loretta through his rear-view mirror.

"Are you comfortable back there?" he asked, laughing. "Normally, I have my grandkids back there. I can't remember the last time I had an adult back there. You're OK?"

We had gone under an overpass and taken a left to get onto Highway 84. A sign for Highway 89 to Buffalo Gap in a quarter of a mile soon came into view, and we exited onto a frontage road.

Loretta responded. "I'm good, fine. Don't worry about me at all."

While Loretta's comfort level distracted us, I thought it best to slow things down, temporarily change the subject. We would get there. We had enough time. We needed to become better acquainted, and I was curious.

"This is really beautiful country, Ken," I said. "You say you were born someplace other than Buffalo Gap?"

Seemingly attuned to what I was up to, Ken smiled at me as we slowed again for another traffic light. I was eager to hear who this man was, what his life was like. Newspapers had reported he was from Texas but not *where* in Texas.

For all those years, I'd only known him as "the hitchhiker."

Ken Robinson

Not only did I have the man's name, but I was also now getting to know the person in the back of Dan's van in 1974. He was originally from Van Horn, Texas, a little town off Interstate 10 about 100 miles southeast of El Paso, born June 1956.

"My mom, Mona Marie, called the area 'the ass end of the world,'" Ken said chuckling. "I'm definitely a child of Texas, always will be! Other than a few visits to Oklahoma growin' up to visit my dad, I've only left Texas a handful of times, one of those you know about."

Like Dan, Ken was the middle of three kids. His brother, Don, was two years older, and his sister, Rhonda, was four years younger.

"Rhonda was born in 1960 when we were living up in the Sweetwater area," Ken said.

"We moved there in about 1958 or '59. Sweetwater is another small town off Interstate 20, west of Abilene. Rhonda's birthday is the same day as my grandma Jennings, my mom's mom, October 1."

Loretta and I exchanged glances. We knew it was purely a coincidence, but there was that date again. I wondered if Ken was tuned into this October 1 thing the same way as me. I wasn't sure how he couldn't be.

"We lost Rhonda Lynn in 2005. She was living in Kansas when she died," Ken stated in a low voice I could hardly hear. "We have no idea how. They just found her one day. She had been dead for a couple weeks.

No one knows what killed her. My brother Don is in Iraq right now working for one of the oil and gas companies over there."

We had turned right on 89 and drove south, passing a business district heading out of Abilene. Seeming eager to change the subject, Ken veered to other memories of his Sweetwater days.

"Don and I were delinquents growin' up," Ken laughed. "One of my first memories was sittin' with Don on our Sweetwater porch shootin' off .22 shells he had pilfered from our dad with a ball-peen hammer. We got about three rounds to go off before our parents zeroed in on the reports. We were yanked by our arms so hard our shoulders nearly dislocated, and then that leather belt came out. Don got it worse being older and the instigator. We never did that again."

As Ken drove, my mind wandered. Kids do some crazy things growing up. Us Walker kids were medium-to-subpar troublemakers. Dan probably got in the most trouble growing up, but I don't recall anything like hitting .22 shells or any other kind of ammunition with ball-peen hammers. This must have been the first of Ken's nine lives-plus he had lived through. I mean, children under five hitting bullets with a hammer? What could go wrong?

"We had guns and ammo in our lives all the time growin' up," Ken continued. "Despite the ball-peen hammer .22 incident, my dad was good about educatin' us about guns and gun safety. Growin' up, we shot about every kind of firearm made. Different gauge shotguns and probably every caliber rifle and handgun. It was in the DNA of a man from this part of Texas. If we didn't own a certain type of gun, one of our buddies did, and we shot 'em all. I've hunted with my buddies all over this part of Texas. I was into the camaraderie of huntin', not necessarily the killin' part."

Ken paused.

"I haven't thought about the connection much, though maybe I have subconsciously. I've hardly touched a gun since 1974. I did a bit of huntin' when I got back and pretended to enjoy it to hang out with my buddies, but my distaste for the killin' part was now amplified a million times. I still have guns, but they are family heirlooms or collector's items. I do a ton of fishin', though, almost every weekend with work buddies."

Ken fell silent. I guessed he was mulling over his feelings regarding guns. A condition not new to me. Others in Dan's life were affected in similar ways. The Bull girls all mentioned avoiding violent images on television for years because it reminded them of Dan's murder. I would say likewise for my sister.

The more Ken spoke, the more his story fascinated me. It was certainly an interesting contrast to what we had experienced growing up.

In Sweetwater, when Ken was about ten, his folks separated and then divorced. It had been a rocky relationship for years. Ken's father made a living as a truck driver. He was also a lady's man and a heavy drinker. He had lived a fast life, perhaps believing his time was limited because he had already lost three brothers—one in the Korean War and the other two in freak accidents.

Ken's mom moved the kids to the Abilene area in early 1967 where friends told her there was great opportunity and a good place to raise kids. They ended up in Buffalo Gap. Ken said he fell in love with the area at first sight.

After the divorce, Ken's dad returned to his hometown in Arkansas where he tried his hand as a plumber. Ken's dad abandoned the plumbing business for unknown reasons and went back to driving trucks, mostly based out of Oklahoma, in the late 1960s. He admitted to Ken years later that leaving Arkansas and the plumbing opportunity was maybe the worst of many bad life decisions he had made.

"There was a period of time," Ken went on about his father, "maybe ten or twelve years, my dad was married off and on to this woman named Evelyn. I think my dad met her in a bar in Oklahoma City. At the time, my dad was working for Transcon Trucking up in Oklahoma. We called this woman 'Evil Evelyn'. I can't describe to you my personal feelings toward that woman. You've never seen an evil female character in a movie who could hold a candle to Evelyn. Evelyn had four kids already when my dad met her, two each from two different fathers."

I put my hand up.

"Wait, wait, wait. Slow down."

Ken paused acknowledging my request for a time-out.

"What do you mean they were married off and on? Your dad legally divorced and then legally remarried the same woman more than a couple of times?"

"Yeah," Ken answered, smiling. "Oh, it gets better. Believe me! I think it was four or five times off and on married to Evelyn. I stopped keepin' track. In between Evelyn marriages somewhere he was married to a younger woman named Sherry. Right after the Evelyn years, he married a woman named Marcy, and he topped it off in the later years of his life with Violet." Ken laughed. "Sometime during my dad's time with Evil Evelyn, up in Oklahoma, she tried to poison all of us."

"*What?*" I exclaimed. My tall tale warning system started beeping in my head.

Ken saw the look on my face, sensed my skepticism, and laughed even harder.

"We are not even to the part where Evelyn draws a gun on my dad and shoots him. I'm tellin' you, you are not gonna believe some of the stuff I'm tellin' ya, but I swear! I swear to you, it's all true!"

"OK," I said, raising my eyebrows and shaking my head, enjoying the ride.

I looked at Loretta and she gave me a smile and a shrug that Ken caught. He laughed again. I was taking a big liking to Ken. He certainly didn't take himself too seriously.

The story that had brought us to Buffalo Gap, Texas, the reason we were with Ken in the first place could be put in the category of fact is stranger-than-fiction. It would be wrong for me to question Ken's wild history, as out of the ordinary as some of it might sound. We had all met people with unusual, stranger-than-fiction life stories. Ken's boyhood, alone, was worthy of a book, perhaps even a movie, with or without the episode involving Dan.

"All us kids, except for Evelyn's oldest who was in Vietnam," Ken said, "were sittin' down to a dinner Evelyn had put on the table. It was unusual for her to put that much effort into a home-cooked meal. It was more often takeout or something much easier. All six of us kids are about to dive in when Dad comes into the room and yells, 'Don't eat! That crazy witch is trying to poison us!' He grabs the tablecloth and pulls the whole meal onto the floor in a clanking, shattering mess of dishes and food."

Ken waved his hands around the steering wheel, indicating the flying mess in the kitchen. "Evil Evelyn had put rat poison in the food. My dad had somehow figured it out and saved our lives.

"Dad loaded Evelyn into the '66 Impala, and they left the house for a few hours. Unspeakable things happened that night and throughout their years together. I shouldn't speak more about their relationship. It wasn't pretty. This was during my dad's heaviest drinking period and most stressful times of his life."

Of course, I couldn't resist inquiring about Evelyn shooting his dad. Ken laughed, shaking his head, and explained that one night Evelyn came at his dad pointing a loaded .22 handgun at his torso. Ken's dad had knocked her hands down, the gun went off, and the bullet hit his foot where there were still fragments to this day.

As we arrived in Buffalo Gap, we veered right. It was a small town that hadn't grown in population for a long time. Ken confirmed that the population hovered between 400 and 600, while Abilene had grown by about a third over the last thirty-five to forty years. Tall oak and elm trees lined the avenues as we entered the little town. A couple of blocks in, Ken took a right onto a road through an area that seemed to have unusually ample parking for a small town. Then he stopped, put the truck in park, and turned to face Loretta and me.

"Trust me, y'all, I get it. It sounds too crazy to be true. The story of my life until things settled down. I'm not sure I have more history as unusual as our time with 'Evil Evelyn,' but there was definitely more antics and angst. My early life was wonderful but crazy. When you are living it as a kid, it doesn't seem out of the ordinary. In my teens, my life got even wilder. After my ride with Dan, things went off the rails and out of control for a number of years."

Ken became introspective.

"I'm a little embarrassed about the level of family history I'm sharing."

I laughed. "Rarely, if at all, do families dodge controversies, Ken."

Loretta jumped in. "So you be-bopped between Mom and Dad for a bunch of years after the age of ten. That must have been tough on your routines as kids?

It was something Loretta knew more about than me. Her parents had divorced when she was in her early teens and lived far apart.

"Routine? There was no real routine in our lives. But for us, no routine was normal. It was great!" Ken answered with a big grin.

"I went to twenty-two different schools. I quit in the tenth grade. I can't tell you how many different places around Texas and Oklahoma I've lived, but it's many more than the schools I've attended. I was smart enough to go back and get my GED when I was twenty-two."

Ken changed the subject.

"See that place over there?" He pointed over his left shoulder at a nice home on a corner lot with a trellised walkway leading to front door. From my initial impression, it seemed there were some nice places in Buffalo Gap. This place, however, seemed even more upscale and well-kept.

"That's that treatment place, that place Oprah brought attention to."

I had no idea what Ken was talking about. Oprah? *What?* In Buffalo Gap? Loretta spoke up.

"I know what you're talking about. I've seen advertisements for it. What's that show called? *Addicted to Food*? That's the *Shades Of Hope* place?"

"Yeah, that's it," Ken nodded.

"Funny that little ol' Buffalo Gap got all that press. I remember seeing what looked like a pretty big entourage there one time on my way to work. I didn't see her, but I expect Oprah was visiting."

After a short pause, Ken added, "I really do love Buffalo Gap. I feel safe here."

Ken put the truck into drive, and we continued our tour of Buffalo Gap and Ken's life.

Dan's opportune upbringing, contrasted with Ken's rough and tumble Southwest Texas early life intrigued me. Dan's routine was comparatively consistent. Plus, through all of life's trials, our folks stayed married.

"I love my dad," Ken said. "He taught me how to shoot pool, dance, and chase girls, all the important stuff."

Ken laughed with a sarcastic tone.

"He quit drinkin' around thirty-five years ago. I took the good in my dad, which is substantial, and let go of all the bad. We have been close and best friends for years. He's my dad! We are all in a much better place now. My dad is not in the best of health these days, but he's still with us, as is my mom. She was and is the rock in our lives. She's very healthy and runs a daycare operation to this day."

We hadn't gone very far at all when Ken again stopped the Nissan on a bridge and pointed down a draw that trailed up to a bluff west of town.

DANIEL *My Brother*

"Almost died out there not long after we moved to Buffalo Gap when I was around ten or eleven. My friend Frankie Richards probably saved my life. Who knows how I lived through that one."

Loretta was the one to bite. "What happened? How did you almost die?"

Ken needed zero encouragement. He put the truck in park again. Something one could evidently do in Buffalo Gap at any time without impeding traffic.

"Around the time we arrived in Buffalo Gap, I talked our dad into sending us money for a couple of horses. We bought a little paint Welch pony named Bubbles for me and a giant ropin' quarter horse we called Starfire for Don. Bubbles was just plain mean, but Starfire was a well-trained competition cutting horse, nineteen hands high, strong and fast. He was a monster! Yet to be beat in a race in the surrounding counties as far as I knew."

"I'm sorry Ken," I interrupted. 'What's a cutting horse? I've never heard that term before."

"You've seen it, I'm sure, on TV, maybe during a rodeo. They're horses trained to separate cattle. It's that skilled dance you see between the horse, his rider, and the cow he is cutting away from the herd."

"Oh! Yeah, I have seen it!" I responded. Loretta and I nodded.

"Anyway, I was ridin' Starfire with Frankie one day. Frankie was on a pony he'd borrowed from a neighbor. That year, if you wanted to find us, you better own a horse and know your way around the hills. I was in my normal ridin' attire, cutoff blue jeans, penny loafers, no socks, and no shirt. Very cowboy-like, you know?"

Ken laughed.

"We would often ride up to the bluffs, hang out, enjoy the view, philosophize about life, and talk about girls we liked. At the time, I was head over heels for a girl named Monta Appleton. Monta is the reason

I went from using oil in my hair to the dry look. She said she didn't like it and that was all it took."

Ken laughed. He laughed a lot.

"Well, Frankie and I were comin' down from up on the bluffs, trotting at a good pace, when Frankie's borrowed Welch pony kicked it up. Starfire, as I said, was a strong horse. Frankie's little pony was runnin' as hard as he could and Starfire was trotting along, staying neck-to-neck with Frankie and the pony. Instead of loosening the reins, which is all I had to do to get the horse to run—"

Ken paused. "Do you guys know horses at all?"

Loretta said. "I grew up off and on, literally, with horses. Doug knows almost nothing about horses and horseback riding."

I nodded but felt inclined to add, "Dan was into horses!"

Ken looked at me acknowledging another link or interest he shared with Dan. It took a few moments for him to steer himself back to his story.

"Well, I should've just loosened the reins and let Starfire go. Instead, I kicked and yelled, 'Giddy up, Starfire!' That little pony disappeared behind me instantly. Starfire was racing strong as we approached the railroad underpass on the trail. Unfortunately, Starfire was all bloated up when I'd saddled him, and I hadn't properly kicked the air outta him. The saddle loosened, and I slid underneath Starfire with one foot still hooked in the stirrup. I was drug on that dusty gravel path about 300 yards. Here I am in penny loafers, shorts, and no shirt. Starfire finally kicked me loose with his back legs."

Ken's narration captivated Loretta and me. He had an amiable way about him. His voice was a pleasure to listen to, and he was a good storyteller.

Ken said, "Most of the details from there are secondhand. I remember seein' red. There was blood everywhere, and I was hollerin' for Frankie.

Frankie was a skinny, puny kid like me, but he put me on his shoulders and carried me back to town. I wasn't taken to the hospital. My mom cleaned me up as best she could, and I was put to bed."

Ken took a break from his narration, seemingly to organize his thoughts for the rest of his story.

"Three days passed, so I was told. To this day, I have no real recollection from the time I saw red, and I was callin' out to Frankie for help. On the third day after the accident, my brother and sister called my mom at work to tell her I was throwin' up and goin' into convulsions. I was rushed to the hospital. I had busted up ribs, a severe concussion, and the doctor said I had a good chance of dyin.'"

Ken paused again.

"This next part is kinda funny, even given the serious circumstances. Once again, I was told this. I have no memory of it happening. Over the next few days while I laid in the hospital, I would every so often wake up, rise up in my bed, and say, 'Hey everybody!' with a silly grin on my face and pass back out."

Loretta and I shared a pained laugh with Ken.

"It went on for days. I sorta remember opening my eyes once to what seemed like half the population of Buffalo Gap in the room. I brought them from cryin', to smilin', back to cryin.'"

Ken shook his head, chuckling.

"After a few days, I came back from the other side, slipped out of my hospital bed, and went to the mirror to check out my injuries. I now understood the reactions of my family and friends. There I was in my hospital gown lookin' like a giant piece of beef jerky. More black and blue than anything. There was a couple of patches of skin still intact. I had two holes in my right temple where they relieved the pressure of my brain on my skull. The whole back of my head and upper back was covered in stitches and scabs."

Ken paused and I envisioned a ten-year-old Ken Robinson seeing his horror in the mirror at the hospital.

"The same day I got out of the hospital, too weak to throw a saddle on Starfire, I grabbed only a blanket and jumped on. I remember everyone comin' out of the house trying to get me off the horse. I just took off and went to where I'd been drug. For me, I figured it was the best way to put it all behind me."

Ken sat quiet for a few moments.

That's some toughness. Literally getting back on that proverbial horse.

"I haven't seen or heard from Frankie probably since the end of that summer when I went to live with my dad in Oklahoma."

"Ken," I said, "knowing what I know and with what you have told us in the short time we have been together, you've got to be one of those people with nine lives."

Ken nodded. "And maybe a few more, maybe many more."

Ken put the car in drive, and we moved on from the bridge, from Frankie and another of the many times Ken's life almost ended.

Ken looked away from the road again for quick eye contact then back to the road. "Y'all doin' OK? Need to stop for anything?"

Loretta and I both acknowledged that we were good.

"OK, y'all's turn. I've been ramblin' like a mad man! You gotta know I'm as curious about y'all, if not more. At least y'all knew about me. I knew nothin', absolutely nothin' about y'all. The only things I knew is what Dan told me that night, which wasn't much and details hard to remember after all these years. Tell me about y'all, tell me about Dan."

He continued. "I was tense about this meeting. I was out with a girlfriend last night. We're not dating or anything. I've known her for years. She could tell I was apprehensive about all this. She was the perfect friend to be with last night. She was very empathetic, which is what I needed. I kept on repeatin' to her, 'I'm not worried about this meeting, but I *am* worried about it.' I guess what I was sayin' was I've been silently wishin' for this to happen for years and now that it was on my doorstep, I got real anxious. My feet didn't go all the way cold, but they got a little cool."

Ken laughed and said, "I'm glad you're here. Real glad! My feet are OK now. Normal temp. Y'all are from Minnesota? I knew you folks were Yankees, but for some reason—it must've come from Dan—I thought y'all were from Illinois?"

Ken, like many folks outside of Illinois, pronounced Illinois using the "s".

He was right. He deserved informational reciprocation.

Down on the Bayou

This broad subject was bound to come up and be of interest to Ken. I probably should have brushed up on our family history before we traveled to Buffalo Gap. How much detail should one share? Where to begin?

Ken had already categorized us as Yankees, which was true. Loretta was definitely a Yankee. She had grown up in New York and Minnesota. We had known each other for a dozen years, married for seven. A first marriage for us both. I was a Yankee, too. I may have been the only born Yankee in my extended family, but I was definitely a born and bred Northerner. Our roots, however, were from Louisiana.

"Loretta and I are definitely Yankees, but my parents are from the South," I began. "My father was from New Orleans and my mother was from a little town north of Baton Rouge, Louisiana. Our parents met at Louisiana State University. My sister Debbie is the oldest, she is nine years older than me. Dan was next, six-and-a-half years older. I was born in '59. Both my siblings were born in Louisiana in 1950 and 1952."

We had inched our way forward in this small town, away from the trail where Ken was dragged by Starfire. Ken stopped again, this time across the street from a one-story wooden building. He rolled down the windows, put the truck in park, and turned the engine off. The building was brown, trimmed in white, and "THE SHACK" was in big white letters above the porch and entrance.

I still didn't know which way to go and how much of our family history would be truly of interest to Ken, but since he'd been sharing a great deal of personal background, I felt we owed him the same courtesy.

We came here for Ken Robinson's story, and he was by far the better storyteller, but I tried to relay to Ken our lives, Dan's life, and how it came to merge with his in the Mojave desert in 1974.

The twists of fate guiding Dan to meet Ken Robinson began in the early 1950s in New Orleans with our paternal grandmother and a locally famous retail musical instrument outfit. Lu Lu Mae Walker was the only grandparent we three kids had known.

Ken raised his eyebrows. "Lu Lu Mae, huh?"

I responded in kind, laughing.

"Yep. That was her name, and it seemed to fit her personality. She was a *lulu*."

Lu Lu Mae was a young, widowed mother with two young children. No one really knew what happened to Lu Lu Mae's husband, our grandfather. They had two kids together, a daughter, Terry, the oldest, and Daniel, my father, three years younger. It was rumored but never confirmed that Lu Lu Mae's husband had jumped off a bridge in New Orleans when their kids were very young and was never heard from again, perhaps because of a cancer diagnosis. If any of that were true, if Lu Lu Mae or any other relatives knew what had become of her husband, it remained a secret. Lu Lu Mae's husband's name was Daniel Ashton Walker, same as my dad, but the junior never made it down or was never taken by my father. To support this little family, Lu Lu Mae worked at Werlein's for Music on Canal Street, the boulevard right outside the French Quarter.

Werlein's was a popular music store and had been in business in New Orleans in some fashion since the mid-1800s publishing primarily sheet music early on. During the first half of the 1900s, Werlein's evolved into a musical instrument retail giant, selling and repairing every instrument under the sun. Werlein's helped support local school band programs and had reach all over that part of the South with stores in Baton Rouge and in Jackson, Mississippi. The base store and headquarters was in New Orleans. I remember hearing stories about Fats Domino purchasing Steinway Pianos from Werlein's and Dr. John (Mac Rebennack) taking guitar lessons at Werlein's.

Werlein's music store on Canal Street in New Orleans circa early 1950s

Lu Lu Mae was a sales lady for Werlein's who traveled the region and worked at their retail stores. She dressed professionally in a blouse, blazer, and a below-the-knee skirt, with about a half-dozen bangle bracelets on both wrists making a ruckus every time she moved her arms. In the evening, for extra money and probably social fun, she played piano at *The Court of Two Sisters*, an old, iconic restaurant in the French Quarter.

Lu Lu Mae did a decent job of raising her kids at a less-than-ideal time, in less-than-ideal circumstances, in a pretty crazy town. She rented an apartment in the French Quarter. Lu Lu Mae never owned a home of her own. I don't think she ever owned a car. She never aspired to be a homemaker—it wasn't her style. My grandmother was an interesting character as I remember. She passed in 1966, when I was seven.

My mom was Leonie (Lee) Becnel Walker. There is documented history on my mom's side of the family going back a long way, all kinds of branches of a family tree. There is a book about her family written in 1982 called *LeDoux*. It chronicles the family going back to the early 1600s.

Our mother had a privileged upbringing in small-town Louisiana. She was the youngest child of four whose oldest sibling was twenty-three years older, one of the reasons we didn't know our maternal grandparents. Her father was a respected doctor in town who died in 1940 from injuries suffered in a car accident a few years earlier. The family did well enough to send their youngest daughter to LSU, where she got a physical education degree and met my father, a man my mom's family joked about being below her social status.

On our father's side, resources for family history were just not that plentiful. My father only had the one sister and she succumbed to cancer in the early sixties prior to Lu Lu Mae's death. My father's sister had three daughters, but they had no additional Walker paternal grandparent knowledge or Lu Lu Mae gossip to share. Lu Lu Mae, I'm guessing, wanted her life private for whatever reason.

My dad attended a boarding school while he was growing up—St. Paul's Academy in Covington, Louisiana. It was a high school across Lake Pontchartrain from New Orleans. I'm not sure if it was for discipline or other reasons that he went to St. Paul's. I get the impression my dad liked to rumble when he was younger, and Lu Lu Mae, a working widowed mother in the 1940s, likely needed the help and some time for herself. Boarding school would've given that extra discipline and male influence that she could not offer. Apparently, she made enough dough to pay for such a school. St. Paul's is still in existence and, oddly enough, during this research, I found a picture of my father on its website as part of the 1943-44 football team.

My father then served a brief stint as a gunner on a destroyer in the Pacific at the tail end of World War II. He would have been seventeen or just eighteen. His birthday was in August, and Japan surrendered in August. Either he enlisted at seventeen or it was postwar mop-up duty. After that, he attended LSU where he met our mother, but dropped out one semester short of graduating. I never understood how one could put in that much time and not get the degree, but there was probably some reason. My guess it was money. It will remain another mystery along with our paternal grandfather's disappearance.

After dropping out of LSU, my father got a job working with my grandmother at Werlein's Music Store. That's where the twists of fate truly begin to form.

I was taking a breath to figure out the quickest path to connect the next historical dots for Ken when he broke in, speaking softly with noticeable guilt and his now-familiar, low laugh.

"That place over there." Ken pointed at THE SHACK, shaking his head. "I've been married four times, twice to the same woman," he said with a chuckle. "Don't ask," he begged. "I repeated some of my father's mistakes, unfortunately, but that place cost me at least two of them marriages. Man, they used to give away their food. They had it all figured out. They would charge almost nothin' for the food, and everyone would come in, get somethin' to eat, then stay and drink all night."

Ken's demeanor changed, facial expression and all.

"It's also the very first place I went after arriving back in Abilene in 1974. My brother, Don, picked me up from the Abilene truck stop. Don said, 'Let's go to THE SHACK and get a beer.' I said, 'No, I can't. I promised God I'd quit drinking.'"

Ken smirked and looked at Loretta and then me.

"I'm not kidding. In those few seconds lyin' in the back of Dan's van fearin' for my life, I made that promise. 'God, please let me live. I will quit drinkin' and lead a better life.'"

Ken shook his head.

"Well, that promise wilted quickly! Don pressed me a little, I folded, and we beelined it back to this place directly from the truck stop in Don's homemade 1958 Dodge dually pickup truck."

Ken paused and took a breath.

"We got real drunk. I was so damn happy to be home. I tried to tell him what happened to me in California, but, really, I get it now. Unless you were there, it's hard to believe much less feel and have empathy about what happened. Don wasn't very interested in my story. So, we just got drunk, and I shut up about it followin' advice given by the cops as I was leaving California."

Ken shook his head again.

"Those were some turbulent times in my life. Oh my gosh! Those two years after that ride with Dan, I 'bout killed myself. Like I said, I'll tell you about that later. Continue clueing me in. How does all this connect with this music store you're talkin' about?"

Ken urged me on, using his hands, but his latest revelation regarding THE SHACK had briefly derailed my train of thought.

"This is fortuitous, Ken." I recaptured my thought process and said, "Much of this is secondhand, but two-weeks-ago recorded secondhand. We also interviewed and recorded one of the few people alive who knows this history firsthand, a man named Bob Bull. He confirmed and added some updated detail to the history I remember."

While parked across from THE SHACK, I proceeded to fill Ken in on our migration to Illinois from Louisiana, the Bull family history, and their close relationship with our family. I could look over Ken's shoulder while I talked, imagining the day he got back from California, broke his promise to God, and worked up a drunk in this little bar in Buffalo Gap with his brother. He had been a very young guy and had been through unimaginable trauma. The minute degree of separation from the nightmare he was part of in 1974 and the folks I was speaking of would become clearer. In fact, Uncle Bob and Ken were probably in close proximity of each other October 1, 1974, when it fell to Uncle Bob to make a positive identification of Dan.

Home

As I continued recounting our history with the Bulls and our family's migration to Illinois, Ken started his truck, put it in gear, and moved on from THE SHACK. I guessed we were continuing our guided tour of Buffalo Gap. It wasn't going to take long to see all the sights. It might take a while to share all the memories, though.

"See that big tree there?" Ken asked, pointing as he drove to a big, obviously ancient oak tree trimmed of its lower heavier limbs over the years.

"When we were kids, there was a huge beehive in that tree, the kind of beehive you see in cartoons. It was huge! Me and a couple of guys took .410 shotguns and blew it away. We got everyone in town stung that day."

"You and your buddies were just roaming Buffalo Gap with shotguns?"

"No," Ken laughed. "We found the beehive, ran home, got the shotguns, and shot up the beehive. We got in a bunch of trouble for that lapse of judgment."

Loretta piped up from the backseat. "Wow, Ken, you were a troublemaker, huh."

Ken nodded. "Yeah, me, my brother, and my buddies probably used up a bit of other folks' nine lives in those days. I'm gonna show you my place and let my dogs out. My place is nothin' to brag about, but it's home for me."

We headed east from the center of Buffalo gap, I think. I have pretty good directional awareness, but Ken had spun me around in this small town. I wasn't driving. I was focused elsewhere, doing more talking than I wanted.

"So you did grow up in Illinois?" Ken confirmed, pronouncing the "s" again.

"Yeah," I replied, nodding. "Pretty much the extreme northeast corner of Illinois, straight above Chicago, less than thirty miles from the Wisconsin border. We were a twenty-minute drive east to Lake Michigan. For me, it was a utopia of an upbringing. I won't speak for my sister or Dan, they were older, but my life from year one to ten was everything a kid could ask for. Other places were called home after that, but we were lucky to spend ten formative years on that property. I believe Dan and Deb would agree with me. They were in high school living an upscale life with abundant opportunity."

Ken took a left onto a dirt road. We passed a couple of homes on the left. The right side was mostly undeveloped. We continued about a quarter of a mile until the road seemed to end. Ken took another left at a dirt road that turned out to be the circular driveway of his home.

"I got this place a few years ago. Like I said, it's nothin' fancy but it's heaven to me. I got the house first and then the property next door not too long after." Ken started laughing. "I'm like that nosey neighbor on Bewitched. What was her name?"

Joining him in laughter, I shouted, *"Gladys Kravitz!"*

"That's it!" he said, laughing harder. "I was home one day and saw the guy, a local car salesman who owned the property next to my house. He was talkin' to another guy. I'm sneaking around behind trees like *Gladys Kravitz* trying to figure out what they were talking about."

I started laughing harder, visualizing Ken sneaking around the property eavesdropping.

"I hear somethin' out of this guy, who I figured was a prospective buyer for the property, somethin' about grandkids, thirty goats, and eighteen cats. I couldn't catch up with the guy sellin' the property at that moment, but I tracked him down early that Monday mornin' at his dealership. I wrote him a check on the spot and told him to tell the other guy whatever he wanted, but I was buyin' that property. I had just made a deal on some custom chairs imported from Mexico that I had finished for a bar owner. I was instantly broke again, but I'd have eaten bologna sandwiches for years before I'd let that property get away from me and into the hands of a budding barnyard."

Loretta and I continued laughing.

"I love my little place. It is truly home for me after so many years of movin' around. I scraped up enough to buy the house in 2002. I have just under five acres. Let's get out and stretch. I'll go let my dogs out."

Ken put the truck in park, switched off the ignition, and jumped out of the truck. Loretta shut down the recorder. We looked at each other, hesitating to move. But if Ken didn't show any concern, we guessed his dogs were friendly to strangers. I got out first, and Loretta followed. Ken went to the house, up the front steps, and opened his front door, releasing his hounds. All three rushed over for a polite sniff then went about their business. Ken retrieved a couple of lawn chairs from under the porch and set them up for us beside the truck. I surmised we'd be staying awhile.

Loretta sat first and hit the record button again. At this point we were only capturing our own words, but Ken had been interjecting, and we didn't want to miss anything he was willing to share.

As the dogs sniffed around the perimeter of Ken's property, he leaned against the truck passenger side door across from where we sat with our backs to the yard and house.

"Sounds like a pretty nice place where you grew up," Ken mused, arms folded across his chest.

"Yes, it was. It was a great gig." I then gave him a rundown of our fortunate upbringing during the sixties.

When my parents invested in the Diamond Lake place, they were just four or five years removed from renting a very modest apartment in New Orleans. They now resided in an "upscale" place on a lake, had a boat, and threw parties regularly for any reason they could concoct.

The Diamond Lake place had seventy-five to one-hundred yards of lakefront with a wooded lot just left of us. A manicured hedge line ran from the wooded lot along half of our lakefront. In between the lake and our house, bracketed by two thirty-foot-high Martin houses, was an oval-shaped pond partly covered with lily pads teeming with bluegills and perch. The lake fed the pond via a lagoon just off our property to the right. If one included the attic and walkout basement, it was a four-story white house on a rise above the lake. It had a huge picture window overlooking the lake with a terrace just below where we held many summer outdoor social events. About ten doors down from ours along the lakefront, the neighborhood had a private beach tucked in between huge oak trees. Our parents added an older used ski boat not long after moving in. Dan and his older sister became proficient water skiers.

From that home, one could monitor the entire north side of the lake. A shallow sand bar with rocks was about fifty yards offshore from our property. My father painted a big fifty-five-gallon drum red and anchored it to the rocks to mark the hazard for boaters unfamiliar with the lake. However, the warning often went unheeded. One of my father's evil pastimes was to drink cocktails on the terrace while watching boats ignore the shallow water marker, ripping up their props. "Oh, well. Hey, Lee, how about another Scotch!"

Our property became a key gathering spot for fun in all seasons. Neighborhood sandlot games of every sort for every time of the year, including summer waterskiing get-togethers. We'd shovel snow off the pond and lake in the winter for pick-up hockey games or skating parties. My parents loved to have Dan and Debbie's friends over to share in the fun of such a great property.

Backyard on Diamond Lake, Mundelein, Illinois. Circa 1961

We kids were guided to be outdoorsy. Young Deb and Dan had explored the bayou with their dad, crawddadin', fishing, and engaging in other Louisianan activities. Those interests continued in Illinois. Dan was once so proud of a northern pike he'd caught off our property's lakefront one evening that he barged in on our mom while taking a bath in order to weigh the eight-pounder on the bathroom scale. Annual long weekend trips to the Boundary Waters in Minnesota added to our adventurous spirit. Dan was the greatest beneficiary of these adventures with his dad.

Looking back, our life on the lake in the sixties was remarkable. But as Ken alluded to earlier, as a kid, it all seems normal. Of course, our normal was quite different from Ken's.

As for Dan, any interest he'd had in organized sports waned after he entered high school. As a freshman and sophomore, he felt he was too small for football, and he'd never had a huge interest in playing other sports. Dan had begun to have other interests: literature, history, politics, travel, socializing, and girls.

When Dan was a sophomore at Carmel High for Boys in 1967, David Bull was a freshman "day-boy" (nonresident) at Lake Forest Academy, a boarding school. That same year, 1967, Uncle Bob and Aunt Connie became part owners of The Homestead Resort in Midway, Utah.

Back in the mid-1950s, Aunt Connie's parents, Martha and Ferrin Whitaker, along with other family members, invested in a seasonal resort in their native Utah that came to be known as The Homestead. In 1967, when a sale for The Homestead fell through and all the other partners had already moved on to other commitments, Ferrin and Martha, unable to shoulder more management responsibility for the operation asked Uncle Bob and Aunt Connie to invest and help manage the property.

The Homestead's history goes back to the late 1800s. Founded by Swiss immigrants Maria and Simon Schneitter, everyone knew it back then as Schneitter's Hot Pot Resort. The two-story brick hotel and swimming pool officially opened in the summer of 1891 and became a destination for travelers and families from the neighboring areas. The resort, on the west edge of Heber Valley, was built around the largest of the many fumaroles, locally called hot pots, in the valley. The Homestead fumarole served as the resort's geological focal point and provided a steady supply of mineral-rich, 90- to 96-degree water to a bathing pool. A second, proprietary spring fed by the nearby Wasatch Range provided water to another, much colder pool. After buying the property, the Whitakers renamed the resort The Homestead and the old hotel The Virginia House, where the Bulls, after investing in 1967, would spend four-month-long summer stretches in the multi-room, multi-bathroom apartment above the main lobby.

The Homestead and Richard Menzies

What age are you when you are the most impressionable? A social scientist or any other kind of scientist, I'm not. I took sociology and psychology classes long ago, but it's not something I've explored since. I suppose it largely depends on your circumstances but one's teenage years must play a huge part in who we become. Dan and his peers turned sixteen in 1968, when America's involvement in Vietnam was at its peak. The Tet offensive that lasted much of the year started the end of January. The black and white images from Vietnam had already been horrifying, the console color TV my parents bought in 1968 only served to make those images from Southeast Asia more vivid and shocking.

Martin Luther King Jr. was shot in early April. Riots erupted in major cities across the United States. In March, President Lyndon B. Johnson announced that he would not run for another term. In June, Robert Kennedy was assassinated. The American political system was in turmoil. The Democratic National Convention in Chicago in August saw 10,000 anti-war demonstrators square off against 23,000 police and national guardsmen. Meantime, Dan and his buddies were about two years away from being eligible for an all-expenses paid trip to Vietnam.

That is unless they could score a deferment from the draft. College was the best option if you had the interest, the grades, and could afford it.

In the summer of 1968, Dan got a job with a neighbor's company. Bill Grasmick lived on our block in Mundelein. I don't know if my father had anything to do with Dan getting the job. He more than likely sent Dan to ask for one. Mr. Grasmick, president of Herschberger Implement Company—the International Truck and Tractor dealer in town on the north side of Mundelein—hired Dan at fifteen to work as a helper and "gofer" in the implement shop. Dan would not have been afraid of work. None of us hesitated to get out and start earning our own money. Dan had already been working hard for eight years helping with lake property chores, and we'd grown up watching people with solid work ethics.

The only negative feedback I ever overheard regarding Dan's first job was an incident involving a forklift, which Dan backed up and nearly knocked a vehicle off a jack onto a coworker. An early safety lesson learned without negative consequences. That job had to have been a good experience for Dan, and it was with someone I remember as a good man and likely an early mentor. Bill Grasmick wrote to Dan in late summer 1968:

August 2nd, 1968
Daniel Walker Jr.
Mundelein, ILL.

Dear Danny,

As I told you when you asked whether we had summer employment, the work would be difficult, hot, and dirty. I have made it a point to watch you do a great number of the latter.

You have learned one thing at an early age, however, that is, the time to hang on is when the average man would quit. Continue that attitude and you will have no problems.

Sincerely,

W. H. Grasmick, President
Herschberger Implement Co.

During that turbulent American year, Dan had a solid year of personal growth given the mentorship, and the employment experience, not to mention the money to do with what one will at that age.

A week after finishing his summer job at Herschberger's, Dan was on a westbound plane to spend time with his other family in beautiful Heber Valley, Utah. Still managing Story and Clark's business and using Utah as his home base for the summer to help manage The Homestead, Uncle Bob scheduled vacation time from work to coincide with Dan's visit. Uncle Bob and David picked Dan up at the Salt Lake City airport and drove over the Wasatch Mountains to their fifty-acre resort. Dan would have two weeks to enjoy the West, the mountains, and new experiences before starting his junior year in high school. He would visit our friends and this breathtaking place during the summers of 1968 and 1969.

David had entered the forty-hour work week at The Homestead soon after his parents had invested and begun spending their summers at the resort. His first paycheck was for mowing the resort grounds on the 7 a.m. to 3 p.m. shift for forty-five cents an hour. He graduated to washing dishes in the kitchen for sixty-five cents an hour. By summer's end, he had risen to "pot boy," scrubbing pots, pans, knives, and cooking utensils for ninety cents an hour while being bossed around by the busy chefs. His alarm clock would go off at 5:30 a.m.—time to report to the kitchen.

The other Bull kids, once old enough, worked elsewhere on the property. As early as twelve, Martha remembered busing tables in the dining room and washing dishes in the kitchen. Later she worked in housekeeping.

Even before the Bulls were part owners, Leslie Bull remembers her first two-week visit to The Homestead. After arriving and seeing the two pools, the mineral rich geothermic fed warm pool, and near Olympic size spring-fed cold pool, she was excited to hit the water. She asked if she could swim and her grandfather promptly handed her a "monster" ice cream bucket and a stick with a nail in it.

"When that pail is full of rubbish," her grandfather said to the eight-year-old, "you can use the pools."

Neither Dan nor Dave was yet licensed to drive, but there was plenty to do and there were other ways to get around. They rode Blaze, a beautiful horse the Bulls owned, and kept at The Homestead. Blaze had what looked like an explosion of white fire running down his forehead to his snout. There were also stables on site where David made friends with the Heber Valley cowboys and where one could rent trail horses if an extra mount was needed to explore the many mountain trails in the area.

The Homestead had bicycles for rent, tennis courts, and a nicely maintained putting green nicknamed "Ferrin's Folly" just outside the dining room. There was a player piano in the lobby that kids played often, driving Aunt Connie and the staff working the front desk crazy. On the way to the pools from the lobby was an old-time ice cream parlor that employed teenagers around Dave and Dan's age. A crew of local young women attired in dirndl dresses worked the dining room and other places around the resort. Then there were the pools where many hours were passed while Dave was on the clock. It was while hanging out at the pools that Dan found a mentor and role model in a twenty-something lifeguard named Richard Menzies, a bohemian figure who had grown up in the Mormon culture but had gone AWOL. When not involved in the many other activities around The Homestead, Dan hung out poolside and philosophized with Richard.

A budding writer and photographer, Richard had come to The Homestead Resort in June the previous year after having been "deselected" from the Peace Corps.

"If not for Bill Whitaker (Ferrin and Martha's son)," Richard wrote, "it's unlikely I would have gotten a job of any kind, since my resume at the time included two notes attesting to my disordered psyche, one from an Army psychologist, another from a Peace Corps shrink. Then there was my degree from Brigham Young University, which in the secular world I yearned to break into had proved virtually useless. In fact, it was a liability.

"At the time, I was thought to be someone who had shucked the trappings of materialism, although the fact was, I couldn't afford anything better at the time. But that didn't bother me—although lifeguarding at The Homestead paid just $1.40 per hour, I was having the time of my life."

A native of Utah, Richard was born in Salt Lake City on the same date as the Mormon church, April 6, but spent most of his youth in Carbon County, 100 miles or so southeast of the city. He had grown up LDS and been ordained an elder at nineteen. In college, Richard had majored in English, graduating with a Bachelor of Arts degree from BYU. Following years of religious indoctrination, he'd undergone what he called an existential breakdown and was in the process of reinventing himself.

"The first thing I did was trade in my little Honda 50cc Cub on a CL77, a bike with the same 305cc power plant as the CB77 that transported Robert Pirsig from a Minnesota mental hospital to a mountain top in Montana. As Pirsig would later note in his book, *Zen and The Art Of Motorcycle Maintenance*, 'motorcycling is therapeutic.' Indeed, after just two weeks spent zipping around Heber Valley on that bike, I was the sanest person in all of Wasatch County."

Richard's quarters, or should I say "squatter's rights spot," at The Homestead was an old bait shop that had been vacant for years. He named it The Homestead Hilton.

The place had no plumbing. It was situated on the western edge of resort property beside Snake Creek over which a footbridge led to a spider infested two-hole outhouse, for emergencies only.

"Being a lifeguard at a resort only 100 yards distant, with locker rooms and showers, personal hygiene was never an issue. Other than a $27 monthly payment on my motorbike, I had no overhead. Waitresses slipped me free food and everything I could possibly need was at the resort. My swimsuit even came from the lost and found bin. A resident washerwoman, Mae Jones, whose shack was a popular gathering spot for 'The Help,' met all my laundry needs. You knew that you had been accepted into Mae's club the day you saw a doll with your name on it on display. These were glass bottles spouting cotton ball heads and wearing gender-appropriate outfits."

Not subscribing to any news periodicals and doing without radio or television in his extremely humble residence, the tumultuous news events of 1967, 1968, and 1969 got to Richard only by occasional word of mouth. Thus, he lived in relative peace and tranquility.

One of Richard's youthful passions was photography, a craft he had pursued since ten. He was the kid never seen without a camera in his hands.

"Wherever I lived, however humble, I always set up a rudimentary darkroom. This included my shack at The Homestead. Fiber-based prints in those days required quite a bit of washing, so I'd often take a tray down to the bank of Snake Creek and kneel there like a prospector panning for gold. On another occasion, I hiked to the resort and tossed my photographs into the cold pool, jumping in afterward to agitate. The artist's so-called 'Chlorine Period.'"

Richard Menzies outside the Homestead Hilton circa 1968
Photograph by Richard Menzies

In those days, The Homestead was only open for business during summer months. Following the 1967 season, Richard ventured north to Utah State University in Logan, where he put in a half year of graduate school until his savings ran out. He rode his motorbike over Sardine Pass in a blizzard to Salt Lake City and worked odd jobs to pay rent on a humble basement apartment in the Marmalade District.

Convinced the happiness he had experienced in Heber Valley during the summer of '67 couldn't be repeated, he resisted reconnecting with former friends and coworkers. That is, until one fateful day in July, he rode his motorbike over the mountain to Heber Valley. As he stood outside the pool area chatting up lifeguard Dee Davis, someone noticed a young boy floating unconscious in the deep end of the warm water pool. Dee appealed to Richard for help, and his instincts kicked in.

"I had never taken a lifesaving course, but somewhere I had read about mouth-to-mouth resuscitation, and to my great surprise, it worked!

As the victim sputtered to life, I was rewarded with the semi-digested remnants of a Homestead burger, followed by an embrace from the boy's father, and, finally, a firm handshake from Ferrin Whitaker."

Thanking Richard profusely for his quick action, saving the resort from a potential lawsuit, Ferrin offered Richard his old job back on the spot. Unanchored to anything back in Salt Lake City, Richard resumed residence at The Homestead Hilton. Dan arrived at The Homestead less than a month later.

Today, Richard is an accomplished author and photographer who has traveled throughout the Mountain West, finding stories where others aren't looking or care not to look. He shot a famous photograph of Burt Munro, who later became an icon of the motorcycling world, thanks to the film *The World's Fastest Indian*. Understated and humble to this day, Richard has stayed near his roots in Utah, and after much urging from the Bull kids, I found him immediately. I'm glad I did. Another person I should have contacted long ago.

Richard wrote in one of his first notes after we connected: "I've saved some of Dan's letters, copies of which I can share. Also, pictures, including one of him at full gallop astride Blaze the Wonder Horse. Did I mention that your brother was also fearless?"

Danny Walker riding Blaze the wonder horse in Utah, 1968 or '69.
Photograph by Richard Menzies

What is a mentor? Ideally, everyone has positive role models in their lives. Mentorship happens at different times in one's life. Sometimes, it's your parent, a friend's parent, or another adult. Teachers, coaches, bosses, and even close friends have impacted my life. Many teens, at that time in their lives, are trying to find their way, and find their voice. Richard was observant, educated, opinionated, philosophical, and a photographer, talents and traits of interest to Danny Walker at that time in his young life.

It was a time when Dan was seeking outside influences. Outside of his biological parents, outside of his other parents, Aunt Connie and Uncle Bob. Outside of the priests and brothers at his Catholic high school. Richard bonded with many people at The Homestead, but especially with my brother Dan. Dan, in the primal stage of teenage rebelliousness, found Richard's lifestyle and low-cost style of living intriguing.

"In spite of my inclination toward solitude, I had quite a few visitors to The Homestead Hilton," Richard wrote.

"Many were teenagers, who looked to me as a different sort of adult—that is, an adult who, like Peter Pan, had never grown up. Among them was Danny Walker, who at the time was struggling to figure out just how he was going to make his way in this crazy world. He often referred to himself as *Holden Caulfield*.

"Like Benjamin Braddock, in *The Graduate*, Danny didn't want to be sucked into selling plastics or whatever. We two *definitely* shared that in common. Hell, Robert Bull even offered me a job selling pianos in Chicago, when all I really wanted was to ride off in a Greyhound bus to nowhere in particular with Katherine Ross by my side."

Danny Walker circa 1968 at The Homestead. Photograph by Richard Menzies.

Richard was, and continues to be, a hopeful and incurable romantic. No wonder he and Dan hit it off.

"I enjoyed our conversations and probably learned as much from Dan as he learned from me," Richard wrote. "In fact, he came up with the title for a book I was destined to write many years later: *Virtue Is Its Own Punishment*.

"Your brother also gave me some good advice in the summer of 1969, after I introduced him to a girlfriend I'd met in Puerto Rico when I was a Peace Corps trainee. 'If you don't marry her,' advised Dan, 'you're crazy.' So, I did as I was told. Anne and I have been together now for more than fifty years."

"Thank God Richard was such a good man," Martha Bull recalled.

The Bull kids and other young Homestead staff (The Help) hung out with Richard around the resort and out at his shack. Martha admitted going on several capers with Richard on the back his Honda despite her parents' anti-motorcycle sentiments, forbidding their kids to ride or own one.

Despite having a counterculture reputation, despite his lifestyle, Richard didn't indulge in many of the habits associated with rebellion. He didn't have his first taste of alcohol until he was twenty-two, a beer, and never partook in recreational drugs.

"I've never even smoked a joint," he confessed when we first met. "Maybe I should have."

During that first meeting at Richard's home in Salt Lake City, he also helped push forward the writing of this book by saying, "If you finish this, Dan lives forever."

Richard added energy to Dan's already growing interest in literature and writing. The two corresponded often after that summer's sojourn at The Homestead. The name Richard Menzies became well-known around our home, even though Dan was the only family member to have ever met him. Upon returning from Utah, Dan immediately set up a darkroom in the attic in the Diamond Lake house and started practicing his new photography hobby. He invited me up occasionally to watch him at work and show me the developing process.

Richard's lifestyle was intriguing to Dan, but I doubt that Richard alone sparked Dan's interest in motorcycles. I'm sure the attraction was already there, despite our parents sharing Aunt Connie and Uncle Bob's disdain for the sport. I would argue that bikes are both a nurture and nature allure. If you have any interest at all, and if ever you can get your hands on the levers of power, it's unlikely you'll ever turn back.

Dan turned sixteen in October during his junior year at Carmel. In February 1969, he started work at National Tea food store in Mundelein in the produce section. Dan worked there off and on throughout his high school years and was always flush with cash, working evenings after school and mornings before school started.

He wrote to Richard Menzies in the spring of 1969.

Late May 1969,

I was hit kinda hard two days before a wonderful summer opened. Barbara Anne Dethorne 1952-1969, May 27th.

She was the best friend I had at school this year. Whenever I was sitting by myself, she was there. I really just met her at the beginning of this year, our friendship grew more and more. I found her to be one of the most delightful nutty and relaxing people to be with. I guess I loved her.

I'll show you her picture someday, a couple that I took, developed, and printed. She was really beautiful, really beautiful.

Dan had arranged a date with Barbara Dethorne for Saturday night. Dan and Bob Schneider had spent the preceding afternoon together, and Bob remembered Dan's excitement about his plans to show "Babs" a good time. "Babs" Dethorne was killed May 27, 1969, two days before the end of the school year near Illinois Beach State Park on Lake Michigan. Walking across a series of train tracks, she misinterpreted a frantic warning signal from an engineer and waved back. An express train hit her going eighty miles per hour.

I felt Dan's grief regarding Babs. Early one morning, music, haunting music, awakened me. It was *One Less Bell to Answer* by the 5th Dimension. The "45" on Dan's record player was on repeat—the needle kept going back to the beginning over and over. I finally got up to see what was happening. Dan had fallen asleep, remembering his friend. I turned off the record player and went back to bed.

June of 1969 saw my sister Debbie on the move. She headed to Europe for seven weeks with a twenty-person St. Norbert group, flying into Frankfurt. I presume Dan, already keen on adventure, was inspired, albeit moving in his own direction.

During her trip, Debbie traveled through Austria, France, Switzerland, Italy, England, and Germany. While traveling the German Autobahn with her tour group July 20, the bus pulled into a wayside stop crowded with hundreds of travelers from countries across the globe. There, all quietly standing, gripped in anticipation, they watched on a single twenty-inch screen television, the black and white images of Neil Armstrong descending the lunar module ladder to the surface of the moon.

"One small step for man, one giant leap for mankind."

She remembered how the international crowd erupted with joyous enthusiasm, hugging, and shaking hands.

We watched Armstrong's historic step at home with Dan and Bob Schneider. It was nice to see upbeat imagery on television for a change.

Bob and Dan went off by themselves that night, parked the car under the stars, and listened to continuing coverage of the moon landing on the radio while speculating about the possibilities as this new frontier continued to open.

"That's the night I came to believe Danny was different. He was a deeper thinker, more philosophical than most. It was a real cool evening," Bob Schneider remembered.

Dan made his second trip to The Homestead in the late summer of 1969. He would again visit the Bulls and reconnect with friends he'd made the previous year.

To Michelle
From The Homestead
August 9, 1969

Dear Michelle,

I have just spent my first 24 hours at The Homestead. I shall proceed to give you a full report on my actions.

I arrived in Salt Lake yesterday at 10:40 Salt Lake time. I proceeded to find myself a chair because I had a three-hour wait in front of me. After about 20 minutes of waiting, a young man sat down next to me. He was dressed up in a cowboy shirt, original Levi blue jeans, shocking yellow socks, and tie dress shoes. He was tall in stature and asked me, in a Western accent, "Where ya goin' partner?" I answered back in the same dialect, "Why I's jus' goin' to The Homestead, down in Heber Valley." He, just as everybody else, had never heard of such a Godforsaken place. We continued to talk of such interesting things like the weather or the very popular "moon shot" etc., until I found a good excuse to leave ... I had to take a piss.

After this episode I roamed the airport until I was met by Uncle Bob. He came in from Chicago on the next flight, and the one and only photographer Richard Menzies picked us both up and drove us to The Homestead.

I unpacked and started to roam the area meeting old friends and making new ones with the employees.

I am suffering from a bad case of saddle sores. I rode two hours up the mountain trail and this condition attacked me just as it would any other "city" boy who tried that after not riding for a year. Needless to say, I'll have an iron butt after two weeks of this.

I miss you very much and it is rough knowing that you are 1,198 miles away. It's rough to have a butt around here 'cause everyone is a Mormon and they crucify people that smoke. Maybe Jesus smoked too. But occasionally, I sneak one in. It's beautiful country, I'll send you some postcards.

With Love,

Danny

David, now in his third full summer at The Homestead, was working long hours and gaining more experience in the kitchen. Richard was back at the pool where discussions of literature, photography, religion, rebellion, and travel continued.

Dave and Dan still had enough free time to play cowboy, exploring the hills on horseback and engaging in occasional, questionable activities. As was often the case, the boys' mischief was instigated by none other than Uncle Bob Bull.

While riding in the hills astride Blaze one day, Uncle Bob had come across, what appeared to be, an old grave. There wasn't a headstone, but it was laid out in a way suggesting a final resting spot. It was in the middle of nowhere and not tended to in any way. Uncle Bob was curious, wondering what interesting artifacts might be buried beneath. Bob Bull was a mischievous soul in his own right, but getting these two young men to execute deeds on his behalf was even more special. It created *teenage mischief plausible deniability.* Plus, it would give these boys a project to keep them "out of trouble." He supplied Dan and Dave with pickaxes and shovels and sent them off to investigate.

It being Mormon country, the site was near a trail that pioneers trekking from back East had taken to the Great Salt Lake Valley and beyond. After days of hard work digging through roots and rocks in the August heat, the boys had nothing to show for their blistered hands and sweaty, aching bodies. Perhaps they hadn't dug deep enough by the time the owner of the property rode up on a horse with his broke-back shotgun at the ready.

They got a severe reprimanding from the landowner who had a previous run in with Uncle Bob. The Bulls longtime family dog had been shot and killed by the sheriff while trespassing on the landowner's property. The neighbor marched the boys down to the resort to make sure their parents were aware of what they'd been up to on his property. Once he had left, Uncle Bob said, "Well boys, I have to punish you for this misdeed. You will not be allowed to use the pool facilities until … well, until tomorrow morning." It was 7:00 p.m., a very chilly night, and the pool was already closed.

After all these years, David told us he'd give anything to go back and dig around those roots and rocks again with his friend Dan.

On Dan's day of departure from Heber Valley in 1969, the crew drove to Salt Lake to put Dan on a plane back to Illinois. His baggage made it aboard, but the plane was overbooked, and Dan could not get a seat. The airline gave Dan a toothbrush and advised him to return to the airport the next day to fly home and reunite with his luggage.

Back at The Homestead that night, Martha, David, and Dan slipped off to Snake Creek to enjoy a bonus night together. Uncle Bob was normally the one who kept close tabs on his four kids plus Dan, but whenever Uncle Bob was out of town or busy with other responsibilities, surveillance fell to Aunt Connie, aka "Colonel Connie."

Hanging out near the Homestead Hilton, mostly just chatting with nothing scandalous going on, Martha, David, and Dan were startled by a bright flashlight approaching in the dark.

David yelled, "Who's that? Turn off that damned light."

The response from behind the light brought the three to immediate attention. "IT'S YOUR MOTHER! What's going on down here?" Aunt Connie demanded. "It's time for everyone to get home. And you!" She pointed at her second son Dan. "Shouldn't you be packing or something?"

The circumstances surrounding Dan's delayed departure from The Homestead hadn't reached Aunt Connie, the busy co-owner of the resort. As Martha once quipped, "Those days when my parents were part owners of The Homestead, I needed an appointment to see my own mother."

"I'm all packed, Aunt Connie," Dan replied, pulling his airline-issued toothbrush from his breast pocket. "I have all my stuff right here."

When Dan left The Homestead in 1969, a doll representing him was on display in Mae Jones' shack. Dan had been accepted into her club despite, technically, being affiliated with "management." Those allied with the resistance were rightly proud of his achievement. The next time Dan saw Aunt Connie, Uncle Bob, David and his three sisters would be summer 1974.

Woodstock happened while Dan was at The Homestead on August 18, 1969. It was another pivotal year in American history and in Dan's life, as well. Entering his senior year of high school, leaving behind his second family and his bohemian friend and mentor, feeling trapped by his parent's expectations, and facing the possibility of being drafted, Dan was at an existential crossroads. Like many young people at the time, Dan had strong objections to the ongoing war in Southeast Asia.

Some are dedicated to their studies their senior year, others-hell bent on having fun. Dan was the latter, but still made good enough grades to get into college.

Whizzing Around with "Wiz"

To Debbie spring of 1970 from Dan

The change is evident. Soon I'll go away to college and Mom & Dad will rub their eyes to see if it is really true. Of course, I will rub mine too in realization of the time that has passed. What the hell happened to the good old days when I played army in our back yard and spent endless summer days at the beach? Tree forts and BB guns, hell, that's all lost in the past. Sometimes I sit and close my eyes and relive them all over but then I open them & try to see what the future holds. Hell, it is a great life.

O'Donnell got his draft notice in the mail the other day. God, it makes me scared.

Based on bestselling novels, satirical anti-war films featuring field doctors during the Korean war and bomber crewmen based on an island off Italy in World War II debuted in theaters in 1970. They were a hit with the public and with Dan. Dan added the soundtracks to our family's broad music collection, hoping our father would appreciate the humor, hear the message, and get the hint.

That spring saw the break-up of the Beatles. Paul McCartney released to the press on April 10 news that he was moving on from the group. The next day, Apollo 13 was launched, and for nearly a week the world was glued to the events unfolding in space.

The Kent State shooting happened less than a month later May 4, 1970. The young woman in the infamous picture of the Kent State shooting was passing through Ohio at the time. Still a middle teenager, she had ended up at Kent State, joining the protests of Nixon's decision to bomb Cambodia. She just happened to be talking to a perfect stranger, Jeffrey Miller, before the shots rang out and she hit the pavement. With his last frame on his roll of film, student photographer John Filo captured the photo of Jeffrey Miller lying dead, shot in the face, and the young woman's reaction kneeling beside his body. Before John could reload his camera, the young girl was gone. Many fateful twists occurred that day. For the young girl, for the photographer, John Filo, and, of course, for Jeffrey Miller and the others who died or were injured. Dan graduated from Carmel High School for Boys later that month.

In August 1970, Dan was seventeen. He wouldn't turn eighteen until October. He had worked all summer, but the summer wasn't going to end without an escape, an adventure, a celebration of post-high-school freedom. It was a roughing-it, see-everything-you-can-in-the-shortest-amount-of-time kind of trip. It was also a chance for him and his traveling partner to practice their photography skills, a hobby Dan had embraced and continued to pursue following his time in Utah with Richard Menzies. It was the beginning of August when he and one of his Carmel High School buddies, Tom Wiznerowicz, embarked on a road trip through the northeastern United States.

Hitting the road at four in the morning, Tom and Dan made it to Dearborn, Michigan, where they spent the day touring the Henry Ford Museum and shopping at Greenfield Village, a historical village of shops, arts, and crafts. By that night, they had crossed through customs into Ontario and were camped on the shore of Lake Erie. (Dan wrote that they bribed the Canadian border agent.)

We caught up with Dan's 1970 traveling partner, Tom Wiznerowicz, after the writing of this book had begun. He and his wife, Mary Ann, named their first child after Dan, Dana, a girl who died soon after she was born. Tom still had a picture he took of his friend Dan on his office wall after all these years. The photo was one of Dan's last gifts to his parents, and it adorns the cover of this book.

"I remember that trip well," Tom said. "It lasted around three weeks, and I don't think we stayed in a hotel but maybe once or twice. We camped or just slept under the stars during the whole trip. We bathed in lakes along the way, and we ate from a box load of canned goods in the trunk that our moms had supplied us with before we left."

That first night, after crossing into Canada, Dan wrote from a "magnificent" bluff in lower Ontario along the muddy beaches of Lake Erie.

August 1st, 1970

We must have the most beautiful and desolate campsite in the whole world.

Even as I sit here and write, the great grizzly bear has just taken off with next month's supply of baked beans. If the poor animal does get them open, I pity him the next morn', after which, he will probably come back to take revenge on Tom and me.

The next day, Tom and Dan headed east again and stopped at Niagara Falls. Dan continued to practice his imaginative writing in his next letter home to his friend Michelle.

Today, we left our little beach on Lake Erie and headed east once again. We stopped in Niagara falls and saw the falls. I watched quite intently as Tom went over the Canadian Falls in one of those Schlitz Beer Kegs.

After the foam had cleared, we found the intoxicated body of Tom floating 5 miles downstream. A Mountie in red, long underwear and traditional Canadian Mountie hat tried to give Tom artificial respiration but soon became too intoxicated to continue.

They spent the day touring the area before camping at another secluded campsite in North Central New York State, then set out the next day to tour and hike Natural Stone Bridges and Caves in the Adirondacks. The massive Stone Bridge is the largest marble cave entrance in the eastern US and is still being carved by the beautiful Trout Brook. They visited Fort Ticonderoga, toured the museum, and watched men dressed in full period uniforms fire cannons during a reenactment.

Now Tom and I after traveling a booming 100 miles are in Vermont on Lake Champlain where we, under cover of darkness, took a stand-up bath in the cold waters.

At a gas station tonight we heard talk of a big storm a-brewing. If the rain falls, this leaky tent will probably not fare so well. So we may leave early in the morn' for Maine to do some horseback riding and fishing.

Today the battery on the car went dead two times and Tom and I had to run about a mile in heavy rain for a jump.

The two young men did, indeed, get up early, and they made it across Vermont, New Hampshire, and into Maine. On this three-week-long expedition, they pulled *On The Road* antics, changing drivers while moving at sixty miles per hour.

Today, Tom and I drove through New Hampshire and into Maine. About 20 miles into Maine, we stopped and went horseback riding in the mountains. OH WOW! It was pretty cool and Tom's horse ran away with him about 10 or 12 times.

Tom had been bitten by a horse when he was eight at a friend's farm, so he was strongly biased against these animals. He believed they were dangerous. Dan pressed Tom into that horseback ride, and Tom capitulated, almost entirely because of the great-looking girl riding the lead horse. Rescuing Tom that day became her primary job.

Afterwards we drove to a little town where an old man was sitting in front of a rickety old whitewashed three-story building. He wore an old pair of blue and white striped overalls and smoked a big old pipe, which almost burned the white whiskers that grew out of his old, battered face.

Screeching the brakes and turning around the corner, we hopped out of the car and snuck around the back of three old buildings, Tom with two cameras and me with one. We snuck around the building and hopped out from the corner. Flash bulbs and cameras went FLASH, CLICK, POP, CLICK, FLASH. The old man quietly muttered something like, "What are you guys, Nippies?"

Tom shyly corrected the old man saying, "You mean Hippies?"

No," the old man said."I don't think I am too hippie."

At this point a young girl in a mini skirt walked by and the old man strained so much to look at her, he fell over in his rocking chair. Tom and I helped him to his feet.

You Nippies aren't all bad," the old man conjectured.

"Hippies," Tom said. "And we are not Hippies."

"No you are not as hippy as that cute girl that just walked by."

Goodbye," we said.

"Bow tie?" asked the old man. "No, I don't have any."

"No!"

"Goodbye, so long, farewell," said Tom.

"Oh, bye," said the old white-haired man.

They headed for North Maine, Baxter State Park, and on to Mount Katahdin (Translation: Greatest Mountain) Baxter Peak. It is the north end of the Appalachian Trail running from Georgia.

Dear Michelle,

Howdy! Well today I had another reason to send two letters for the price of one. Tom and I got up at 4:30 to go take pictures of moose in the park. We walked about two miles to a lake where the moose were supposed to water, sat for two and a half hours and saw nothing, not even a chipmunk.

So we decided we would walk up to Baxter Peak, the highest in Maine. Well, we started to walk along this path and got tired of the old beaten trail and started up our own way trailblazing. Dumb move! We were walking through evergreens, dead pines, and birch trees, getting all cut to pieces, when we hit this 90-foot ledge. We worked our way up the ledge which took about an hour. When we got up to the top of the ledge we were no nearer to the top of the mountain than before and all we saw *were evergreens, dead pines, and birch trees. After about four hours of climbing we were hot, tired, and sweaty.*

Tom finally agreed to turn back only to figure out we were about 20 miles from the car and didn't know how to get back. Well anyway, we started back and practically stumbled down about 10 miles of mountainous forest with thousands of flies going after our hot sweaty bods.

At about 3:30, we got back to camp too tired to do anything except to take a stand-up bath in the lake, unveiling about 100 cuts apiece and blisters galore. We gently walked out into the water. The soap hurt all the cuts and the stones popped all the blisters. You might list today as a failure except for one thing. Last summer a lady and ranger died up on the mountain we were at by making the same dumb mistake we did.

Call you Friday or Saturday.

Me

"We had this goal to climb anything that was climbable!" Tom recalled. "We weren't competing against each other to see if one person could make it and the other couldn't. We were pushing ourselves to see and accomplish as much as we could in three weeks on a very tight budget."

Postmarked August 9, 1970
Friday the 7

Dear Michelle,

The Atlantic! We finally made it to the Atlantic, 2000 miles and we are camped on the Atlantic Ocean. We are in Gatherings Campgrounds, four miles south of Ellsworth, Maine. About 20 *miles ago, Tom and I stopped at an old run-down barn that had been converted into an antique shop. We browsed around until I came across an old beat-up hunting knife just like the ones Daniel Boone, David Crocket, and James Bowie used to carry. I immediately fell in love with it and bought it for $10. You will have to see this baby to believe it. Tom bought an old Spanish wine jug complete with homemade wine. When we sat down to dinner, chili, bread, crackers, and fruit cocktail, Tom hauled that monster out and we had a glass full... don't know what it was, but ever since I drank that stuff I have had the worst stomachache!!!!!!*

Tomorrow we will move on probably all of the way to Cape Cod. We might get a motel room there, a real live bed. How 'bout that. I'm down to about $100 and fading quick. I don't believe in prayer, you do ... pray for me.

I'm really glad that I am on this trip. I always wanted to go out alone and see the country ... it's nice, but I wouldn't like to live like this.

I inherited the knife my brother bought, the one just like the ones Daniel Boone, David Crocket, and James Bowie used to carry. I wore it often while exploring the outdoors in the late seventies until it slipped off my belt in a pit toilet at Starved Rock State Park in Illinois or Devils Lake in Wisconsin. I felt a terrible loss even though, by then, I had grown accustomed to letting things go, almost as a badge of honor.

Dan's letters to Michelle stopped after he and Tom reached Maine. Maybe Dan ran out of paper, out of energy, or out of time. They were moving fast and furious, and it didn't sound as if they slept much during their three-week-long trip. Tom was able to provide some of the missing push pins of their itinerary.

The two young travelers went south to Boston and to the North Church Tower, where on April 18, 1775, Sexton Robert Newman and Vestryman Captain John Pulling Jr. climbed the steeple and held their lanterns as a signal to Paul Revere that the British were marching to Lexington and Concord by sea across the Charles River and not by land. The American Revolution was underway.

Dan and Tom visited Bunker Hill, the *USS Constitution* in Boston Harbor, and Plymouth Rock while working their way down the eastern seaboard to Provincetown, on the extreme northern tip of Cape Cod, where the Mayflower landed in 1620. They did a drive-by past the Kennedy Compound in Hyannis Port.

"We were hitting as many historic sites as we could find," Tom said. "The small towns and sea shores in New England were captivating. We were having the time of our lives."

Dan purchased a harpoon while visiting New England, not far from Nantucket, across the bay from where Herman Melville's *Moby Dick* begins. That harpoon once prominently displayed on our mantle over the fireplace in Libertyville found its way to a corner in the basement after 1974.

The pair continued across Rhode Island into Connecticut, home to the Museum of America and the Sea in Mystic, Connecticut. It is the largest maritime museum in the United States, notable for its collection of sailing ships and boats and for the recreation of the crafts and fabric of an entire 19th-century seafaring village—a visit that could only have contributed to Dan's lofty dream of sailing the world.

"We made it to New York City," Tom remembered.

"We made it downtown to the Empire State building, but the traffic was horrendous, so we just drove by and got outta town."

The picture of these two young men driving through New York City with a harpoon sticking out of their car was memorable. They were starting to run low on money and time but continued to visit historical points southward.

"We caught the Liberty Bell in Philadelphia on the run," Tom said. In Washington, DC, they visited and climbed every monument. After paying their respects at Gettysburg, the pair headed for home, arriving in late August from the road trip of a lifetime, much less a young lifetime. Dan was still seventeen. He packed and, with great reservations, went off to start college at St. Mary's in Winona, Minnesota, a picturesque town in the upper Mississippi River Valley.

The Attempt at College

God bless the people who know exactly what they want to do growing up, whether that includes higher education, military service, or another ambition. Also, kudos to those who go on to higher education knowing upon entering the career they aspire to. It's not like that for many. It wasn't like that for me, nor Dan.

Dan thought working and travel would be the better teacher, at least at that point in his life—knowledge gained through exploring the world, meeting new people, and seeing it through the eyes of others, living simply on a budget, photographing, and writing about his experiences along the way as his friend and role model he'd met in Utah two years earlier had been doing.

In our home, though, the pursuit of higher education was expected. Our parents viewed college as essential, and with us kids working to help defray the cost, they firmly planted in our minds the idea of college from our earliest days. My father had a strong will, so Dan, choosing the best option possible to avoid conflicts, both in Southeast Asia and at home, went off to school in Minnesota.

While those born in 1952 hadn't yet become eligible for the draft lottery, Dan found himself cornered by expectations and circumstances.

He likely felt he had learned more on the road the last month than he would learn the whole next year in school. Practical, social, historical, geographical, geological, and budgeting lessons were all part of his trip through the Northeast with Tom. He understood the importance of formal schooling but wasn't fully committed to it at this time in his life.

Dan's buddy John O'Donnell and another good high school friend, Jim Fitzsimmons, had been working and planning a year-long, low-budget trip to Europe. I don't know under what circumstances Dan's friends missed out on a trip to Vietnam. Perhaps their lottery numbers were high, or they had a medical or another deferment.

Given the hindsight of decades, historians and political pundits have certainly questioned the wisdom behind our country's involvement in Vietnam. However, in 1970, when Dan was eighteen, evidence of how the narrative had been manipulated by our government was only gradually becoming clear. Returning soldiers who had loyally served were now joining the ranks of civilian protesters in questioning our continued presence in Vietnam. After nine years of conflict with no end in sight, the anti-war movement was moving at full steam.

Assassinations had rocked America's world two years earlier, along with the Tet Offensive. The Kent State shootings and Woodstock had helped amplify the beat of the anti-war movement the previous year. The My Lai massacre in March 1968 had just become public in November 1969 and had sparked further criticism of the war, especially among younger people, including Dan and most of Dan's peers. The spirit of the younger generation had undergone a seismic shift. They didn't want to participate in "general's bingo" and be forced to fight for a cause they now believed to be false. None of them wanted to be the next man, much less the last, to die in Vietnam.

If Dan had been turning eighteen earlier in the sixties, before Americans had learned how those in power had distorted the truth regarding Vietnam, I'm convinced he would have loyally served if school hadn't work out. He wasn't afraid to serve, fight, and perhaps, die—he was against killing for a cause that, by 1970, American youth seriously questioned.

The battle in Dan's mind, as he went off to Winona, raged. He was envious of peers who had taken off in other directions unencumbered by parental expectations. Literature influencing him at the time also pushed him away from "structure." School! School! School! Our parents expected all their children to pursue higher education, yet Dan's most influential friends and favorite authors were champions of nonconformity.

Dan consistently pushed the rebellion envelope with his father. Not out of disrespect or on purpose. It was a battle of wills. A battle common in the late-sixties and early-seventies between fathers of the World War II generation and their postwar progeny.

That autumn, major changes were also taking place at home. Consolidation in the music industry accelerated, and another company acquired Story and Clark Piano Company. After fulfilling contractual obligations, Uncle Bob accepted a similar role with another industry player. The Bulls had moved to Tennessee, and there were strong indications that our father would follow his friend to his new company.

Assuming he'd soon be working with Uncle Bob's new organization in Tennessee, our father listed the Diamond Lake property in Mundelein believing it would be difficult to sell. News whether we'd be moving to Memphis was repeatedly delayed. When someone made an offer on the lake house, my father tried to stall the potential buyer for as long as possible. Then, three days after he finally accepted the buyer's offer, the employment opportunity that may have existed with Uncle Bob in Memphis disappeared.

We packed up in January 1971 and moved to the next town over to everyone's unspoken dismay—not as much dismay for my parents, as it meant they'd no longer be living in the red. But from my *Wonder Years* point of view, the house on Diamond Lake had brought us good luck, and from the moment it sold, it seemed to me, our family's luck began to change. Just as I've had recurring dreams about Dan for years following his death, I've dreamed through the years about that idyllic place on the lake.

Dear Ma and Pa,

Wow!!! I am eighteen years of age. You guys may feel different, I don't, but the years have flashed by me all too fast. But the things I can remember!!!! Bathing au natural in a mud puddle. My first day of kindergarten. I believe I was dressed in my best blue jeans and my very best T-shirt, if you don't believe this, look at my kindergarten picture. When I walked down those stairs at St. Francis, I had to take one step at a time, just like Doug used to do, or else fall down all 13 of them.

I brought my first friend at Santa Maria home. He had a crew cut, fairly dark eyebrows, green eyes, and long eyelashes. His name was John. Mom, I think you were in the kitchen vacuuming. The house was dark and so big I used to get lost, but then I found myself.

There were years of backyard football and baseball. Fishing in a pond and a father that would do it all with me if he could.

Now I am in Minnesota. I have been gone the longest I have ever been. Now once again, I wear blue jeans and T-shirts, and again I am lost, hopeful to find myself.

I miss my family and HOME (not house) in Mundelberg. I do not cry because I know they will be there if ever I get my spirits down or if I need a hand to pull me out of some quicksand that I am slowly sinking into. Thanks for my 18 years. If I could tell you guys on paper how much I do miss and love you, I would.

All my love,

Danny Ashton Walker

October 15, 1970

Dear Michelle,

Wow, if I died today my whole life would shoot before me. It would probably go by so fast I'd ask for an instant replay. I hope sometime soon I can find my direction in life and stop running half-assed all around the damned country and do what I really want. Which might just be running half-assed all over the country. Or maybe practicing medicine in New Mexico with a bunch of Spanish kids.

St. Mary's was a great school in a beautiful part of the country, but it wasn't working for Dan. Debbie's advice that autumn was to come to visit St. Norbert and see if it was a better fit. So, Dan hitchhiked from Winona, Minnesota, to De Pere, Wisconsin, a 220-mile jaunt through the central part of the dairy state. His last ride that day was from a doctor who picked him up in central Wisconsin. He and Dan hit it off so well the doctor ended up buying Dan dinner and going out of his way to deliver the young traveler safely to the campus and Debbie's residence.

Dan probably didn't want to be in school at all, but with his older sister's urging he decided to transfer to St. Norbert at the end of the fall semester 1970. He wasn't finding his groove in Winona and being at St. Norbert would be more convenient and less costly. Our parents agreed it was a good idea, especially in view of the other changes taking place.

As we prepared for our move from Diamond Lake, subtle events throughout that fall gave me the impression that our fortunes had taken a turn. Then, as we wrapped and packed the final household items, a sudden gust came, a larger example of our changing winds.

Deb had missed out on our local relocation that January, having joined a ski trip to Colorado over her holiday break with another St. Norbert group. She got back just in time to put Dan's stuff into the back of our Oldsmobile and head back to school with the help of John O'Donnell, who had volunteered to drive the family car back from northern Wisconsin before he left for his trip to Europe.

Mom was managing the final details of our move as Dad traveled for business. One late detail included a last-minute sale of the boat. As Mom was negotiating with a potential buyer at our front door, a rattled Deb called to say that a tractor trailer had jackknifed at a stoplight and hit Deb, Dan, and John on their way out of town. Had the truck not jackknifed, everyone in the car likely would have been killed. They were lucky in that they were sitting three across in the front bench seat because the truck crushed everything in the trunk and backseat. We joked afterword that the guy buying the boat finalized the deal with our mom without further negotiation out of pity. By the time the wreckage had been cleared and the move had settled in January 1971, Dan was in his second semester of college with Deb at St. Norbert, and we were living in a new home on a quarter-acre lot in Libertyville, four miles distant but worlds away from the house on Diamond Lake.

Back in school that spring semester, Dan's life was relatively peaceful and uneventful, even as his hair grew longer and his opinions louder. Home for the summer, he set up a basement darkroom with walls inscribed with graffiti: "DO YOU EVER WONDER WHY PEOPLE WONDER?" and "BECAUSE OF THE LACK OF INTEREST, TOMORROW HAS BEEN CANCELLED–God." The unusual decor made me laugh and gave me things to think about at a young age.

On August 5, 1971, the draft lottery for men born in 1952 took place. Dan was at a party with his buddies for the event. The highest lottery number called to report from that lottery would be 95, meaning all young men assigned that lottery number or lower would be classified 1-A: eligible for possible induction. Dan's number was 75. It was good he was in school.

Even as the drawdown from a high in 1969 of 550,000 Americans deployed "in country" had begun, young men were still being sent to a war never declared, and protests against the war continued to mount.

The holiday season of '71 in Libertyville was highlighted by a small but very out-of-control party December 21, as my sister announced her engagement to a man she'd met at St. Norbert. Dan was off doing his own thing and was not present for this event. Maybe a good thing. He'd seen enough family insanity over the years.

Our Battle of the Bulge veteran, Uncle J.C., his wife, daughter, and son-in-law were in town for the celebration. In a display of jubilance, a wine glass throwing contest erupted. No one could hit the active fireplace from the dining room fifty yards away through the kitchen. Even to a twelve-year-old—the physics didn't seem to work—even if they had been sober, the ceilings higher, and their projectiles more aerodynamic. We found glass shards for weeks following that evening's festivities.

The last thing I saw that night before going to bed, shaking my head in fear of what I might step on or find come morning, was my New Orleans native uncle on my brother's 205-centimeter Kastle snow skis perched at the top of our second-story stairs, tips hanging over the edge. I don't remember if he made it down the stairs on skis that night. I just know that my battle-hardened uncle was confident he hadn't yet used up all nine of his lives.

With her announced engagement, Debbie was on track, meeting all parental hopes. She would complete her degree at the end of the semester and had plans to marry Denis Terry from Baraboo, Wisconsin, a fellow graduate of St. Norbert and a state senator's son.

The winter/spring semester of 1972 was different for Dan.

Letter from Danny to Deb early 1972.

I know very little about the feelings that might be & probably are inside of you now. If love were the Boy Scouts I'd be considered a tenderfoot.

There are many places and things I have seen in your life, all of these things made you. Changes are frightening but inevitable. Sometimes we crash into them as if we were thrown through a plate glass window.

Others came as easy as opening a very elegant looking door with your name written on the door knocker.

The things in the past are not gone, changed but not gone.

For me & my experiences I think when you find love, you become one & fulfilled through one another.

Before that school year, Dan and Deb went in on an older model green MGB convertible for $600. Dan was likely influenced by Uncle Bob, who had bought a new one a few years earlier. Dan's and Deb's car would barely start, even on mildly cold winter days, much less the below-zero days of Northern Wisconsin. Moreover, the MG leaked oil. It was a poor choice given the latitude and Dan's level of mechanical know-how.

There were many frigid winter mornings when Debbie, needing to get to her student teaching assignment across the Nicollet bridge into Green Bay, couldn't start the car, nor get her younger brother, who'd likely been out late, out of bed to help.

"Danny was trying to save the world, and I was just trying to get to student teaching," my sister once quipped.

So, a frustrated-but-determined Debbie had often been forced to hitchhike to work. One of the times she'd had to thumb a ride, Bob

Skoronski, a former offensive tackle and future Green Bay Packer's Hall of Famer, picked her up and delivered her safely to her student teaching job across the Fox River up to Green Bay.

Dan's roommate Rick recalled, "It was an intense year. It was the height of our most intense time at St. Norbert. Danny took everything we were doing and doubled down on it. If we were protesting the war, Dan did it more often and more intensely. If we were experimenting, Dan was going to get the full experience. At the same time, he was out to save the world. Our time at St. Norbert was right out of a movie, a very soul-searching time of life. We were out to find America. 'What does it all mean?' Vietnam was very unpopular. Friends were going over. Everything was confusing."

I visited St. Norbert with my parents late that winter and stayed in Dan's dorm room. My parents were in town for a sorority dinner dance for my sister. Dan would have been an afterthought, as was I, dumped in Dan's bed that night with a book. Being in my older brother's dorm room at thirteen in 1972 was cool. There was a huge American flag dividing the room, representing protest, as well as patriotism, not to mention providing some dorm room privacy. Dan was out partying that night. I awoke in the morning with him wrapped around me in his bed.

My sense was that if Dan wasn't finding his niche in school, he wasn't about to waste my parents' money, even though my father would have invested any amount of money to keep his kids in school for as long as they chose to attend.

April 27, 1972

Dear Mom and Dad,

I have had a confusing year in school, scholastically and personally. Some of my old goals have been thrown out and some older ones have been brought back, with some new ones.

I don't know what I would do with another year of school. It's hard for a person to work at business and accounting courses if he's not interested in business or accounting.

I was trapped in school because of the draft and thought that I had to finish school now, which I feel you would also like to see me do. But I don't think I can go to school until I find some direction. The Conscientious Objector status, which I was hoping to get, would have eliminated one of those problems, and the other ones would have to be discussed.

If your feelings are that strong against the C.O., I will comply with your wishes. I feel that I must also say that my feelings have not changed.

I have already made many mistakes and had a few successes. I am the things that I am. I love you both and respect your opinions on the mysteries of life, which you have come to understand in your way, and I am willing to discuss, not argue, at any time.

I will comply with your wish to drop the idea of the C.O. Don't worry. I am working at it. Someday we might possibly understand each other fully.

All of my love.

Your son and friend,

Danny

Dan's letter only helped to stir further discord. Dan Junior had solid arguments, albeit colored with youthful naiveté. It must have been frustrating for our father. They were both right, and that's what made everything go horribly wrong. Patience wasn't my father's number-one positive trait. He was from the old school, which dictated a by-the-book path to success that mandated a college degree. Moreover, a college deferment was the best way to steer clear of Vietnam.

Those conversations, sometimes heated between father and son, yielded one undeniable truth. Dan was honest to a fault. He had a pressing need to share his thoughts, opinions, and experiences with loved ones, no matter the consequences. Dan went home and shared his spring adventures and experiences at school with his father. Dan's friends were shocked.

"There are certain things your parents don't need to know."

Dan Junior treated Dan Senior too much as a peer, trying to get him to see the world differently. That wasn't going to happen. As his younger brother, I learned from observation that some things were better left unsaid, at least until you get to that stage of laughing about it together later in life as adults. But Dan was in a hurry. He needed to say what was on his mind and in his heart, perhaps knowing he was just passing through, quicker than most.

This fed into the narrative that "Danny died because of drugs," I believe. Dan came home from his sophomore year at St. Norbert having experimented more than his fair share in psychedelics. His friends said Dan *got the full experience* during that spring semester. It was the reason many of them left De Pere after that year, including Dan: to get away from that environment and get on with the next stage in life, whatever that might be.

Drugs didn't alter the trajectory of Dan's life. No doubt that happens to some people, but it didn't happen to Dan. He experimented, it was a helluva ride, but then he throttled it back.

Dan's passion for travel had nothing to do with drugs. The literature he read, stories from friends who traveled the world, his role model in Utah, and a natural urge for adventure nurtured by his father is what fueled it. Those are the catalysts that sent him winging it around the country and the world. What killed him was simply bad luck.

Danny wasn't a drug addict any more than any of us who pushed the party envelope in college. The zany characters who accompanied me during my high school and college years all went on to become doctors and lawyers and such, as well as bankers, salespeople, business owners, photographers, writers, and every other profession under the sun.

None of the Bull kids believed that Dan had a drug habit, problem, or addiction. Martha didn't smoke pot. She had tried it, didn't like it, and it made her fall asleep.

"The only time I partied to any excess with Dan was in Mexico the weekend before he left, and it was tequila," Martha recalled.

Leslie, who never indulged in alcohol or drugs, told us she never saw evidence of drug or alcohol problems with Dan.

Dan's close confidant Bob Schneider thought Danny had experimented, perhaps a tad more than his mates, but then quit and moved on. He also remembered his conversation with Dan upon his departure from school.

"Dude, how do you walk away from college? You'll lose your deferment! What are you thinking?"

Dan's reply: "Bob, I just can't do this anymore."

The "this" was school, the experimenting, and the intensity of the anti-war movement he and his friends were part of that year. He needed a change of direction. His circle of friends were leaving for similar reasons. That reason being everyone was growing up. After bolting from St. Norbert, most of Dan's friends from school transferred to other universities that fall, but Dan had other plans.

Until now, being a student not only got Dan a deferment from the draft but a respite from heated arguments at home regarding the same. But now that his deferment had expired, Dan was 1-A. Dan's view of the war wasn't going to change. Many of his contemporaries were taking drastic measures, moving to Canada, going underground, or pretending to be unfit at preinduction physicals. Dan's first choice was to be reclassified a Conscientious Objector. However, C.O. deferments were only being issued on religious grounds.

My father's view of the Vietnam war and the potential consequences of his firstborn son being drafted aren't 100 percent clear to me. I'm guessing his stance involved duty, honor, and country first—not to mention the embarrassment of having one's son labeled a draft-dodger.

As my sister said in passing one night when I asked her to revisit the period, "There are things I want to remember and things I don't."

That's probably why it's taken me longer to recall an incident lasting only minutes that became the root of my father's guilt about Dan, justified or not.

Chef Carl's restaurant, off Route 176 in Libertyville, was one of our parent's favorite hangouts in the early seventies. They even recommended Chef Carl's when Debbie's future in-laws were looking for a venue for their wedding rehearsal dinner. Chef Carl's had been an enjoyable place for dinner while we were living in Libertyville until the early summer of 1972, when the feud that had been brewing between my father and Dan came to a head.

Dan had recently returned from St. Norbert. His hair was shoulder-length and the dreaded MG he and my sister had bought was leaking oil all over my father's pristine suburban driveway. Not long before, Dan had opened up regarding his experiences at school that spring and was dropping out.

My passionate father was normally a cheery consumer of alcohol, but all of his suppressed emotions rose to the surface that evening. Had Dan's life not been cut short, the rift between father and son would surely have healed. Dan would have become an adult, likely successful in whatever endeavor he chose, and the two would have laughed it off.

Sadly, that didn't happen. If ever our mother blamed her husband for what happened to Dan, it was born of that night's outburst.

Returning home from a nice suburban Friday night cocktail-laden dinner at Chef Carl's, my father stormed in and exploded.

"Get your long hair out of here. And get your fucking car out of the driveway!"

So, Dan did. Next we heard from him, he was in Denver.

My sister and I had different seats to this event. Mine was as it happened in the kitchen, hearing language seldom spoken in our home. Dan briefed his sister in a heart-to-heart in the dark while sitting at the ninth hole of a par three golf course down the street after she got off work. The next morning, Dan set out for Denver crammed into the MG with John O'Donnell and Jim Fitzsimmons who had recently returned from their year-long trip overseas. The trio had a buddy from Carmel who had moved to Denver and was attending Regis College. For a few years, Denver would become a base for a core group of friends living on University Avenue.

Dan wasn't in Denver for long that summer. He worked odd jobs there with "Fitz" and John O'Donnell, hearing stories of their trip overseas. Dan and John started saving money and planning another overseas adventure.

In late summer, Dan returned to Illinois as the family prepared for my sister's September 30, 1972 wedding. She had asked Dan to be a groomsman. Dan lived at home during that time, commuting to downtown Chicago for a job pressure washing soot off buildings. It was a filthy job that introduced Herbal Essence shampoo into my life. Dan would come home from his job barely recognizable, stinking, and covered in soot head to toenail. He would go directly to the shower and, *poof*, my Herbal Essence-scented brother would emerge from the shower, mostly free of soot.

With both working, Dan and my father were able to limit their exposure to one another. Dan tried to be out of the house as much as possible. However, as Debbie's wedding approached, the length of Dan's hair became an issue once again, leading to another, albeit smaller, conflict. With strong intervention from the bride-to-be, Dan finally agreed to a haircut. They both cried as Debbie volunteered to cut Dan's hair. The wedding was another over-the-top Walker celebration. First to arise the next morning, I found my father sleeping face down on the living room floor in his tuxedo.

Derrel's House

Ken had been patiently listening while monitoring his dogs, who obediently stayed close and on his property.

"My place here got washed out back in 2002," he said.

"My kids, my friend, Derrel, and his sons all helped me clean up from the five feet of water that devastated my place. They also helped me raise up the house like you would on the coast so it wouldn't happen again. I have a sizable creek that runs around the edge of my property. That was one of those 100-year floods, but now I'm prepared for the next one."

Ken stretched and said, "Let's take another ride." He called his dogs and they obediently trooped up the steps to his front door back into the house. We climbed into his truck, took a right out of Ken's driveway, another right at the end of the dirt road, and headed toward downtown Buffalo Gap.

"We're gonna go out near Abilene State Park and Abilene Lake, and I'll show you my good friend Derrel's house. He's goin' through some tough times these days."

It's not like there was any agenda for our time with Ken, but I hadn't expected to go visiting and socializing. This was a sensitive subject, and our continued conversation wasn't something I cared to share with strangers. Having just met Ken in person that morning, I had a faint bit of concern, but I'd felt no bad vibes at all, quite the opposite.

However, I worried that adding new players would hinder our exchange of information and distract us from our mission. I reminded myself how hard this had to be for Ken. Should we get sidetracked, we'd just stay longer into the evening, if Ken would still have us.

We zipped through town and headed southwest out of Buffalo Gap. A few miles outside of Buffalo Gap, we turned onto another dirt road that ended up being a long driveway leading to a nice one-story home. Dozens of old oak trees umbrellaed the driveway and property. Ken pulled the Nissan in front of the garage attached on the left side of the house, put the truck in park, and switched off the key. It looked like a river or creek skirted the backyard, hidden by more huge old oak trees. Maybe it was Abilene Lake, I didn't know. We had no idea where we were. Ken opened the door and jumped out of the truck. Loretta and I looked at each other puzzled, unsure if we were supposed to join Ken having received no verbal instructions. Loretta turned off the recorder and we climbed out of the truck.

"This is my buddy Derrel's house," Ken stated as we all met at the front corner of the truck. Loretta and I followed as Ken continued around to the front door.

Without knocking, Ken opened the door, and we entered the home. Ken closed the door and led us toward a large room behind the garage. The party room, a guy's room, in the center of which stood a regulation-sized pool table with space to shoot without obstruction. Along one wall was a rack for pool cues and some empty shelves, the obligatory bar along the opposite wall. On the far side of the room was an open door leading into the backyard.

Ken introduced us to Derrel, his two sons, Zach and Dustin, and Derrel's stepson, Chance, who all acted as if they expected us. I was still unsure exactly what was going on, but it soon became clear that Derrel's house was another of Ken's safe places, where more long-suppressed memories could be revealed.

"Hey, Zack, can I get a cigarette?" Ken asked one of the boys while helping himself to one from a pack on the bar.

"Chance just got back from Iraq," Ken said.

We thanked Chance for his service, hung around, and made small talk with the four men before once again, without invitation, we followed Ken out the open back door of the party room and into the backyard. Off to the right was an unused, probably never to be used again, caved-in swimming pool. I wasn't about to ask, but it appeared that a breakup and a move was in the works. The place was definitely lacking a woman's touch.

We moved to a picnic table away from the clatter of billiard balls. Loretta and I sat side-by-side on the table part of the picnic table with our backs to the man cave. Ken remained standing, his back to the trees and the lake. Loretta set the recorder on the table between us and hit the record button.

"I haven't had one these in a long time. I quit a bunch of years ago." Ken tapped the cigarette on his thumbnail to pack it. A veteran-smoker move.

"Ever since I got that call a month ago from Greg Myler, I've been a little more on edge. You may not know this, but after all this happened to Dan and me back in '74, the detectives drove me to a truck stop on Interstate 40 the next evening. They found two truckers goin' through Abilene and got me a ride all the way to Texas from California. As they were leaving me with those two truck drivers, they tell me, 'Don't tell anyone about what happened, don't say a word. Those bad people are still out there, and they will hunt you down and kill you.' Their warning put the fear of God in me. I have been in a pseudo witness protection program ever since."

I vaguely remembered the detail Ken was referring to regarding the truckers. It must have come via word of mouth from my father. It was something that struck me as odd even at fifteen. Really! You put a traumatized, eighteen-year-old eyewitness to a brutal murder in a truck with strangers? I understand budget constraints but that just seemed wrong.

Ken was still nervously tapping the cigarette against his thumbnail. That cigarette was going to be firmly packed. I surmised he had bummed the cigarette but not the light.

"Here's another thing," Ken said. "I'd called home to Buffalo Gap when I was in the custody of law enforcement early that first day after we got to Needles. I don't think they were limiting my phone calls or anything, but it was the only call I made while all this was goin' on with the police."

Ken rubbed the dirt with his boots, his smoke still awaiting a light.

"My mom was in the hospital and Grandma Jennings was in from Sweetwater helping out and stayin' with my just turnin' fifteen-year-old sister Rhonda. I think I mentioned earlier, October 1 is Rhonda's birthday and also Grandma Jennings's birthday. They were having a little get-together. Don was there too. Pretty sure he was goin' through a divorce at the time."

"Ken?" I interrupted. "Can I ask the reason your mom was in the hospital?

"Sure," he answered. "She was in for a hysterectomy."

I shook my head. "My God! Our mom was scheduled for the same procedure the morning of October 2. She was already at the hospital all day October 1 going in for surgery the next morning."

Ken shook his head. I think he was beginning to feel the same weird, coincidental vibes I'd been feeling all day and over the last month.

"Sorry for interrupting, Ken," I said. "Please go on about your phone call from the cop shop in Needles."

Ken nodded and said, "It was birthday girl Rhonda who answered when I called that afternoon. I say to her, 'Rhonda, now don't tell Granny,

I don't want her to worry. I need you to be strong and be a big girl now 'cause what I'm fixin' to tell you ... '"

Ken stopped his own story.

"I don't know why I said that about my grandmother. She was the strongest woman I ever knew.

"I told Rhonda, don't let on to anything I'm fixin' to tell you, but I'm involved in a murder, and I'm callin' from a sheriff's station in Needles, California. Before I could go any further or into any detail, my brother, Don, grabbed the phone from Rhonda."

Ken had stopped tapping and was holding the unlit cigarette between his two smoking fingers, his index, and middle fingers. His hand was shaking.

"My brother and I, we literally fist-fought all our young lives. I'm talkin' the real thing. Bustin' our lips up. He broke my nose once. We both had our jaws wired shut from brotherly blows to the face. We 'bout killed each other growin' up.

"I tried to explain my situation to Don. What he said next, I didn't expect and I wasn't prepared for. I will never forget his words. He goes, 'Well, that'll teach your fuckin' ass for goin' off to California, won't it?'"

Ken paused, his cigarette shaking in his fingers.

"I hung up on Don right then and there without sayin' another word. There was no sympathy or help comin' from the home front. I had to figure this out all by myself. No mom, no dad, no brother, no one was swooping in to help me with this nightmare."

I thought, *Wow!* once again. The news had reported that a young guy was with Dan, but we didn't know much more than that he was there in the back of the van and gave the first accounts of that morning. How alone that young man must have felt at that moment with no support coming his way.

"That had to be brutal, Ken. I can't even imagine being in your shoes," I said.

Loretta added, "You must have felt pretty alone."

Ken said, "Yeah, I gotta admit that was a tough moment for me. I hung up and I just started cryin'."

Ken paused, drew a deep breath, and continued.

"I turned around from the phone on the cop shop wall after hangin' up on Don. There was a big bench where all these highway patrolmen, the sheriff, whoever the heck it all was. They were all sittin' there as I finished my call. I think the whole morning was coming out in those tears. I looked at those cops and pleaded with them. 'Don't y'all pin this on me! Please, don't y'all pin this on me just to say you solved this case. Do not do this to me!'"

Ken tapped the cigarette a couple of more times on his thumb.

"They tried to assure me that wasn't gonna happen. This one guy, highway patrol I think, he goes, 'Son, we're not going to pin anything on anybody.'"

The tapping continued. That cigarette might be undraggable, it was now packed so tightly.

"This one cop took me to an office. We were sittin' there talkin', and he was still kinda interviewing me and tryin' to settle me down at the same time. He gets a call, I think from a superior officer, maybe it was one of the detectives, I don't know. He's like, 'Uh-huh, uh-huh. I thought that too. There's no way, there's no way.'

"I knew what they was talkin' about. That was before I took the lie detector test or any other serious interrogation. I wished someone had been a fly on the wall and had seen what happened out on that freeway and what I tried to do for Dan."

Loretta and I were both speechless. This was extremely relevant to us and our project, with details and raw emotion one doesn't get from reading old police reports or news articles.

Loretta mustered up a comment.

"My God, it all must have been horrific. It's unimaginable what you were going through."

Ken nodded as he took the few steps to the door of the pool table room and held up his cigarette for a light. Derrel came over with a lighter, lit Ken's cigarette, then disappeared inside. Ken came back to the picnic table, taking a deep drag off the finally lit smoke.

"This is all so weird," Ken said. "This is all a mindblower. When I read one of the reports you sent more recently about this witness that I didn't know anything about."

Loretta and I blurted in unison, "The beer truck driver?"

I added. "Macias?"

Ken exhaled.

"Yeah! I didn't know anything about him. All this, everything is new to me. I had no idea until the other day that there was another witness or that they'd put him under hypnosis to try to get more information. I didn't know any of this stuff until last week. I left California all those years ago thinking I was the only witness."

Ken took another drag and exhaled a long trail of smoke.

"Some of those letters you sent me and the other information you sent early on, about a month ago, unfortunately, I couldn't read because of technical issues. My computer was on the fritz, and it all came over as gibberish. It was unreadable. I've only read the stuff you've sent in the last few days or so since I got my computer fixed.

"Please," Ken implored, "tell me everything you know about this other witness. What he knew. What he told the police. I was able to read some of the reports you sent but give it to me again. You probably know it by heart?"

After the last year and especially the last month, I did know the details pretty much by heart, as did Loretta. But now, another thing was becoming clear. No one, including law enforcement, had kept Ken up to date after the murder. There was no need. He wasn't critical to the investigation. He was not a family member or next-of-kin. He was a witness who police might have called if they had arrested someone. But they never brought in any suspects.

Ken had indicated his lack of knowledge over email and phone and during the last couple hours, but it was just now sinking into my brain. This is *all* new to him. He knew nothing of what we knew. I, we, had mulled through information periodically over the last thirty-six years, looking at pictures of Dan, reading old headlines and reports. Ken got in that truck to Abilene not forty-eight hours after his experience at mile marker 73 on Interstate 40 near Kelbaker Road in 1974, and no further information, not even a picture of his driver, had made it his way until this last month.

Ken took a pull off his smoke. I didn't know how he wasn't passing out. As an ex-smoker myself, I would have gotten dizzy, done a pirouette, and probably faceplanted after two or three nicotine hits. Pool balls crackled behind us.

"Ken," I tried to carefully ask, "let me clarify this so that I understand completely. From the time the detectives solicited truckers to take you away in '74 and told you to keep quiet about this until a month ago, you didn't know if Dan had a family? Didn't know any details of the investigation? If anyone had been caught? If anyone cared? You didn't know anything at all?"

Ken shook his head. "No! Nothing! Period! Like I said, nothing until a month ago when Detective Myler got in touch with me. Then I got in touch with you, and you started sendin' me stuff. It was all brand new to me. All I ever knew was the name Dan Walker. That's it! That was every bit of information I had, a name with no other detail. A name that has been with me forever. I only knew him for about eight hours, but I have spent the rest of my life with him. Or, he has with me."

I was in awe of what Ken had endured. Imagine going through the most traumatic event in your life, turning the page, and never getting another morsel of information and hardly ever talking about it again. It would be that proverbial bad dream that, after a while, was indistinguishable from what was real because it would be absurd if it were true.

"I read something in the paper way back then, while I was livin' in Abilene," Ken said. "It was about a man and a woman who were shot on the side of the highway. I can't remember where it happened exactly. One of the victims survived, crawled to the highway, and got help. Reading about that incident and seeing the similarities to what happened to me and Dan prompted me to call the California cops. I thought that maybe, just maybe, that similar violent act would have some bearing on the investigation into what happened to Dan. It was probably six months or so after I got home to Abilene."

Ken took another drag, exhaling through his nose. The smoke wafted around him.

"I carried a business card that Frank Bland, San Bernardino County Sheriff, had given me while I was in custody. I kept it in my wallet for years."

That card in Ken's wallet was probably the one item from that day in his life he could pull out every so often to prove it wasn't all just a bad dream. I remembered Frank Bland's name too. It was on top of the police bulletin, the BOLO (Be On the Look Out) dated October 11, 1974.

"When I made that call to the San Bernardino police back then," Ken said, "they really didn't take me very seriously. They asked a couple of times, 'Who are you? What is this regarding?' I was never put through to anyone, and I never got a return call. I never called back after that day. I carried that business card in my wallet until finally it fell apart."

Ken shook his head again. We were all quiet for a few moments.

"Please tell me more about this other witness, the truck driver. I really want to hear the whole thing the way you know it. I'm very interested as you might imagine."

I cleared my throat. "According to police, at about 5:30 a.m. that morning, which, if accurate, is within an hour of your encounter with the bad guys, a beer truck driver stopped to help two guys stuck in the desert sand west of Ludlow, on Interstate 40."

"Wait, wait, wait. Step back just a second to the waitresses," Loretta implored, touching my forearm.

"That's right," I nodded and said. "This is really important, too. There is information from the investigation that I haven't sent you and is hardly published outside of Dan's file. It was new to us! We learned this at the same time we learned your name. There were others who believe they saw the killers earlier that morning."

Ken's eyes affixed to mine. "All this time, I thought I was the only witness with information," Ken said. "Now you're telling me there are a few more?"

"Yeah," I replied. "Two waitresses at the Ludlow Café, a little place about a third of the way east from Barstow on your way to Needles, say they saw the murderers early that morning. The Ludlow Cafe is pretty much the only place to eat in Ludlow, especially overnight. Hell, Ken, it's one of three old buildings at the exit in the middle of nowhere, in the middle of the Mojave.

"These two waitresses say they served two customers at about 2:30 a.m. Their description matched the men you described from the crime scene. The early morning restaurant staff described the two men as 'lively.' I'm not sure, but I took lively to mean either boozed up or drugged up or both. The police found these two ladies after canvassing all the businesses along Interstate 40 between Barstow and Needles, the day of and the day after Dan was killed. The two 'lively' men finished their meals and left, the waitresses said, in a gold van."

Ken's eyes lit up again. The original description of the culprits and their van had come from Ken. He knew all about the van.

I hesitated for a second to gather my thoughts. "Hang with me on this next set of facts, Ken," I cautioned. "Its puzzling how the killers intersected with you and Dan. They left Ludlow and actually drove west, not east. Not in the direction you and Dan were traveling. What time do you think Dan pulled over to rest? Do you remember?"

Ken thought for a second. "Man, I'd say 3 a.m. or something close to that. I was asleep for a while after we stopped. I can't be sure, though."

I paused then said, "I'm trying to figure out if you crossed paths with the killers more than once. For instance, did you pass them when they were still eating at the Ludlow Cafe and before they got stuck or did you pass them when they were stuck? You didn't stop to try to assist anyone stuck in the sand, did you? You don't remember seeing anyone stuck and trying to wave you down for help? There is a theory that you passed them when they were stuck, and they got pissed off you didn't stop to try and help. Then when they got unstuck and happened upon you on the side of the road, did they decide to get even?"

Ken shook his head. "No, absolutely not! We didn't stop to help anyone, and I don't remember seeing anyone stuck. Dan may have, but, as I recall, it was just a quiet night of drivin.'"

I nodded and said, "If your 3 a.m. estimate is correct, it's possible that you had already passed going east before the bad guys got stuck. It's just a thought, Ken. I think the police dumped those theories long ago. To this day, the top motive was robbery. Two guys randomly trolling for targets."

Ken nodded that the payback theory didn't make sense, and I was relieved to rule out this motive—which was not to say Dan was killed for anything more. I continued with details etched into my brain, clearer now having visited the various scenes a month earlier.

"The killers drove west from the Ludlow Café and for some reason tried to cross a median near Lavic road on Interstate 40 when they got stuck in the Mojave sand. I don't know if they were heading west on the frontage road or on the interstate. It doesn't matter. They got stuck.

"Now, them headed west? Does that mean they made a mistake because they were intoxicated or were they trolling for victims in that direction first? I have no idea."

Ken wasn't speculating, just listening. He obviously had no idea, either.

"So, this beer truck driver, Macias, was driving eastbound enroute to Needles in the Lavic Road/Ludlow area on Interstate 40 when two white male adults stuck in the ditch flagged him down. Macias described the vehicle as a 1968 or 1969 gold or brownish-gold Chevy or GMC van. Both of the men were in their early twenties, and one was wearing a red bandana around his head."

Ken nodded. "Those are the guys!"

"The guy with the bandana told Macias they had been using a shotgun to shoot posts, vegetation, and whatever other items they could find to get material to put under the tires for traction. Macias pulled over to help these guys get unstuck from the Mojave sand at about 5:30 a.m. That location isn't that far from where you and Dan parked, about thirty to forty miles."

This news transfixed Ken. He had been there, yet this level of additional detail had never reached him.

"They also told Macias that they had recently traded in another vehicle and acquired their gold van in Whittier, California, and they were driving to Indiana. Macias said the one guy referred to the dude with the bandana as Sam. Whether that was made up or not, I have no idea. I would think a cold-blooded killer on the prowl would use a made-up name."

Ken nodded in agreement without adding anything.

"The truck driver, Macias, remembered something else. He thinks it was Sam who was trying to get back to Indiana in pursuit of an ex-wife or girlfriend and his child. After helping the two get their van unstuck, Macias continued his route to Needles at a slow speed because his truck was fully loaded. Near Kelbaker turnoff, which is near where you parked, Macias remembers seeing you guys, you and Dan. He saw a blue and white VW van parked on the side of the road. Then, as the beer truck driver was coming into Needles, the guys he had helped in the gold van passed him still going east, waving as they passed. Macias wondered at the time what had taken them so long to get to Needles. There really isn't any place to stop between Ludlow and Needles. It was puzzling to Macias.

"There is quite a bit to unpack here, Ken. Macias passed you while you guys were still sleeping, otherwise there would have been a ruckus going on. The killers must have pulled off on one of the few exits between the Ludlow area and your location, again, maybe trolling for victims? Got back on the highway after Macias had passed, stopped to visit you and Dan, did their deed, and quickly got back on the road."

Between Ken, the waitresses, and Macias, police had gotten a description of the suspects. But Ken was the first witness. It was primarily his input the authorities used for the BOLO bulletin regarding the two killers.

> **Suspect One** – White male. Early 20s. 5'10". 180/190 lbs, shoulder length sandy blond hair and clean shaven. Wearing a light orange T-shirt with some type of design or insignia on the front. Possibly wearing a bandana type headband
>
> **Suspect Two** – White male. Early 20s. 5.5/5.7 tall. 150 lbs. Dark brown hair, shoulder length. Possible wearing

Levi Jacket and Levi pants. Dirty in appearance. Possibly wearing a bandana type headband.

"I have always wondered, if these guys were the cold-blooded killers they appeared to have been, why didn't they kill and rob Macias? Courtesy for helping them get unstuck? Macias was probably carrying a fair amount of cash on him. If robbery truly was the motive for Dan's death, I just don't get it."

Ken was shaking his head in equal disbelief. "I don't get any of it! Man. It all just makes me sick to think about people doing things like that."

I said, "The investigators believe they got a partial license plate number and the colors of the van's tag through hypnotizing Macias, but that information has always seemed dubious to me."

There was an interval of silence while we digested our recent exchange. My stomach churned after revisiting the details we knew of the murderers.

"Ken?" Loretta asked, breaking the short silence. "I'm sorry, can we step back for a second? I'm really curious. How did you end up in California in the first place? How did you end up at Cajon Pass where Dan picked you up?"

Ken took a final drag off his smoke, which he'd been holding more than smoking. He dropped it onto the ground and snuffed it with his boot. He smiled at Loretta. He seemed relieved to change the subject.

"God!" He said, laughing. "That's something else I haven't thought about for a long time. All the other events have always dominated my mind about that trip. It's an interesting story how I ended up in California and equally crazy how I ended up where Dan picked me up."

Getting to Cajon Pass

The story we were about to hear made me even more grateful that we followed our instincts and found this man.

Ken was in Irving, Texas, living with his dad the summer of 1974. His dad was between Evelyn marriages. The Buffalo Gap-Abilene area was the closest thing to home, but Ken had been moving back and forth between numerous places in Oklahoma and Texas during the early 1970s. He quit school in the tenth grade and admitted to getting a solid street education from his older buddies and his dad, eagerly joining his father at pool halls, dancing clubs, and other establishments.

For money, Ken worked in the automotive department at a discount center, where he became friends with guys who shared interests.

"Bob Hatcher and Tommy Sanford worked in the garden center," Ken recalled. "Bob, Tommy, and I hung around with each other in those days, and they were my rodeo friends, my bull ridin' buds."

"What! Riding bulls? You could use up nine lives in an afternoon participating in that sport," I said with maximum sarcasm.

Ken laughed. "I've done a lot of crazy things. I was this young, wild daredevil willin' to try just about anything, especially if there were girls around to impress. A couple of beers always helped, too. More often than not back then, the riskier, the better. I don't really know why. Just constantly testing fate. Howlin' at the moon, I guess."

Ken paused, smiling at Loretta. "Loretta, pardon me. I'm gonna digress further, but I'm gettin' to your question. We're talkin' rodeo now. That was my passion as a younger man. Let me dance down memory lane a little."

Ken and his buddies were young rodeo fans who frequented Kow Bell Arena in Mansfield, Texas, a thirty-minute drive southwest from Fort Worth. Kow Bell Indoor Rodeo was a famous institution around those parts during the sixties, seventies, and into the eighties, holding rodeos every Saturday night.

While hanging out around the chutes one night, suggesting he could ride a bull for the full eight seconds no problem, having never been on a bull in his life, the competing riders who overheard his bold statement called his bluff. Next thing he knew, there was loaned bull-riding gear in his hands, and he was being led back to the corral to pick out a bull.

"I tried to pick the smallest bull in the corral," Ken said laughing. "I picked one that was kneelin' down eating, but when he stood, I saw I'd made a bad choice. He was a monster! When I climbed on him in the chute, my legs didn't really reach around his ribs. His back was so broad, and I was this skinny kid, my legs stuck out like I was doin' the splits. I could barely get my spurs in the proper place for the ride."

Ken spread his arms to simulate the position of his legs as the chute was about to open. He had Loretta and me riveted.

"All rosined up, sittin' on that bull, feelin' him get angrier and angrier, I must have had the fear of God in my eyes. This total stranger jumps up and goes, 'Don't let any air get between your balls and the bull's back!' Best advice I got that night!"

All three of us broke out laughing.

"I rode that bull all the way out, all eight seconds," Ken said, smiling. "I was lucky as hell. I started fallin' off to the left, and the bull hit the railing on that side and knocked me back on. He spun, and I started slipping off his right side, and the railing knocked me back on again. I could hear yellin', 'Let go! You're gonna die!' I'm lucky I didn't die."

Ken laughed and nodded in my direction. "What number life are we on?"

I laughed with him, shrugging and shaking my head.

"I was hooked on rodeo," Ken said. "I rode my first *three* bulls all the way out!" Ken had a big grin on his face. He beamed at Loretta. "My dad was in the stands at Kow Bell with a bet on me for my first jackpot rides. I got thrown from a big black Angus bull that night and also from a bareback paint. Now that's a dangerous event. Horses kill their riders! Usually bulls only maim."

Wow, I thought, I was so naive! I'd always thought bull riding was the most dangerous event at a rodeo.

Loretta, less of a stranger to horses, laughed. "Yeah," she agreed. "Horses make things personal."

"That they do!" Ken agreed, nodding, and laughing.

"That paint, he backed out of the chute and threw me straight up. I landed so hard my hat compacted on my head. I shoulda broke my neck. I wasn't on that horse long enough for someone to take my picture."

Ken paused, still laughing about his rodeo days.

"Anyways, thanks for letting me digress. Tommy Sanford, my buddy from work and rodeo buddy, was the reason I was in California."

Ken's friend Tommy had joined the Air Force summer 1974. He was supposed to report to Castle Air Force base in Atwater, California, a town between Modesto and Fresno near Merced. The base closed in the mid-nineties. Tommy had bought a brand-new Chevy Silverado pickup truck and needed a copilot to help him drive his new vehicle to California and report for duty. In return, Tommy would give Ken some of his initial paycheck from the Air Force, and he would fly home or take a train. Eighteen, with some money saved, and up for an adventure, Ken quit his job and packed his gear: a change of clothes and other essentials in a double-bagged paper bag, and his bull riding gear in an old beat-up blue and white bowling ball bag borrowed from his mom. To top it off, Ken sported a new, silver belly gray Tennessee Gambler's hat with a brown hatband. Off Tommy and Ken went in Tommy's Silverado to California, Ken with his high-end luggage, looking like a fugitive from a country music song.

"I took my bull ridin' gear everywhere I went," Ken said. "You never knew when you might hook up with a rodeo, have some fun, and maybe pick up a few bucks in prize money."

My admiration and empathy for Ken grew—admiration for the adventure he had embarked upon and empathy for what I knew was going to happen.

Upon getting to California, for unknown reasons, there was a problem with Tommy's pay from the Air Force. They had little money between them, spending everything they had getting to California. Ken had been counting on Tommy and the Air Force to get him back home.

"Bad trip plannin', I know, but I was eighteen and wingin' it. Don't judge me!" Ken said with a wry smile.

After trying but unable to sneak into the mess hall, Ken described surviving on bags of potato chips, Baby Ruth bars, and water for about two weeks. Tommy was able to sneak few morsels from the mess hall for Ken, but he was losing weight he didn't have by the hour.

"Where did you sleep? You weren't going to get away with sleeping in the barracks, were you?" I asked.

Ken shook his head.

"No way in the barracks," he laughed. "I slept in Tommy's Silverado. It was pretty comfortable. I would sneak a barracks shower and clean up whenever we thought I could get away with it."

Tommy's pay continued to be delayed, but the two scrounged up $20 between them.

"I was a pretty good pool player, not great, but I could hold my own," Ken stated. "I had learned from my dad, hangin' out in bars. I took that $20 and turned it into $60. I went to the NCO (noncommissioned officers) club and beat every airman in there who was willin' to challenge me. I took their money and tried not to drink it all up that night."

The next day was when Ken decided to try to use his hard-won $60 to try to get back to Texas. His buddy Tommy took him to the train station but found sixty dollars wasn't going to get him all the way back to Texas. They didn't bother checking on a bus because Ken hated buses and assumed it also would not get him all the way home. That night he had made up his mind. Get one more decent night's sleep in Tommy's truck and start hitchhiking the next day.

"Man, if I do have nine lives, I burned up a few of 'em on that trip," he sighed.

The following day, Tommy took Ken to the front gate of the base. Tommy thought he was crazy, but Ken assured him he was a veteran hitchhiker and not to worry. He had only made a few short hitchhikes around Abilene and Buffalo Gap, surely never anything farther than a hundred miles or so at one time. Not seeing any choice, Ken began his journey about 8:30 that morning with his extra clothes in a fresh paper bag and his bull-riding gear in the blue and white bowling ball bag.

Ken laughed.

"The human mind, the way it works, amazes me. I remember as I was climbin' outta Tommy's truck that morning that Moe Bandy's *Bandy the Rodeo Clown* was playing on his radio. How does anyone remember details like that?"

Ken was pacing a bit but mostly faced us telling us his story. His memory of the day hitchhiking was surprisingly detailed given the years gone by, not to mention the other memory-disrupting event of the next morning.

His first ride that morning was in a maroon Opel Cadet. The guy was already drunk with a cold six pack of Budweiser tallboys at the ready. At that moment, Ken didn't care. He just needed to get home.

"'You want one?' he offered me. I said, 'Suuurre!' I 'bout drank 'em all because of the way he was drivin', running people off the road, and drivin' like a damn fool. I was scared, but I needed to get back to Texas, so I held on, drank his beer, and hoped I would make it to my next ride. That crazy person let me out at a mixmaster, I had no idea where. As I'm climbing out of the car and the Cadet's door is shutting, I'm asking, 'You sure this is the way?'"

Loretta looked puzzled, as was I. Mixmaster?

"Is a mixmaster a cloverleaf?" I asked.

"Yeah, a cloverleaf," Ken confirmed.

Ken remembered rides from an old man in a pickup truck and a black guy who cruised deserted desert roads. He dropped Ken off in the middle of nowhere. The sun had set, and he recalled watching his last ride's taillights for a long time as they disappeared over a mountain. There was very little traffic. He was alone and edgy. It was pitch dark, in the middle of nowhere still very far from home.

Ken's last ride that night before meeting Dan was from a bunch of young kids in a white van. They seemed pretty clean-cut, not troublemakers. They were going into the mountains to party and invited Ken along.

"I said, 'No, thanks. Everything I own, I got on or is in these bags. I need to get home to Texas.'"

The boys in the van let Ken out on an overpass without a cloverleaf.

"I suppose you should expect a bit of this while hitchhiking because you have no control, but again, it felt like them boys dropped me off in the middle of nowhere. I kept tellin' folks I was on my way back to Texas and, for the most part, I was trusting my internal compass and my rides to keep me movin' east."

It was completely dark. The only light was the light of the moon slipping through the nighttime clouds. The freeway passed underneath Ken and his first assessment was traffic was very light. He was prepared to be stuck at that spot in the dark for a good part of the night. It was a steep embankment to get down to the highway, so he needed to steady himself with one hand. It took two trips to get his two bags down the slope, dodging sagebrush and tumbleweed-like vegetation as he went. He was probably lucky not to have stepped on a snake or put his hand on a cactus.

"Once I got me and my stuff down to the highway," Ken said, "I gathered what wits I had left, moved my stuff about 100 yards north of the overpass, and stuck out my thumb. I was cold and not feeling very optimistic."

Envisioning Ken's hitchhiking odyssey in '74 wasn't difficult. I had done a fair amount of hitchhiking as a younger man, mostly during my early college years. I once hitchhiked with a high school and college friend from Macomb, Illinois, to Des Moines, Iowa, to see friends at Drake University our freshman year in college. That trip was about 250 miles. It was definitely safer traveling as a tandem, and it was really only two highways to get to Des Moines, one of them being Interstate 80.

To get home from college in October, also during freshman year, I hitched alone from Macomb to our home in Libertyville, Illinois, about 300 miles. It was a little more complicated. The only thing notable about that trip, about that day, had nothing to do with hitchhiking. It was Friday, October 21, 1977. News was coming out that the evening before, Lynyrd Skynyrd's plane had crashed—the "Freebird" had fallen to the ground.

Nothing scary happened during those freshman year hitchhikes, but I was under no illusion about this mode of travel. I never told my parents beforehand that I was traveling by thumb, but I didn't mind them finding out after the fact. Were they to ask, I wasn't going to lie to them, but I wouldn't advertise the fact, especially after what had happened to Dan.

There's no doubt that I was being hugely, selfishly cavalier. I was making a statement to myself and the world that what happened to Dan wouldn't make me less adventurous and afraid of what might be lurking around the next corner. I was giving the finger to fate, confident that lightning couldn't strike our family twice.

On a short hitchhike of just a few miles in Melbourne, Florida, in 1978, I jumped into a vehicle without assessing the situation. The driver, a younger man, spoke incoherently with his right hand under a towel, a detail I stupidly didn't notice until after the door had shut behind me and we were on our way. Truly in fear of my life, I turned my body to focus my attention, readying myself to defend against any scary moves on the part of my driver. I broke into a cold sweat. Something was dreadfully wrong with this ride, and I wasn't going to stick around to find out what it was. I had to yell, threaten, and show serious aggression to get the driver to stop and let me out. I never voluntarily hitchhiked again after that night.

You're wired while you're hitchhiking, watching every car, wishing, hoping the next car stops and picks you up. Someone cool, someone safe. You know this mode of travel has inherent dangers, but it is exhilarating as well.

Ken had already been on the road that day for what must have been ten, maybe eleven hours or more. It was September 30, 1974.

Ken said, "I don't think I had been standing there in the dark with my thumb out but for a few minutes. I don't remember for sure, but I don't think I had seen a car go by yet. Then, out of nowhere, this blue and white VW van starts slowing down. It was Dan, your brother, stopping to pick me up."

Ken paused again, brushing his boots over the ground in front of us. There was a murmur of conversation from the boys in the pool table room and the drone of an airplane passing overhead.

"I need to go back there! I told my daughter that the other day. I need to get some money together somehow, and I'm goin' away until I find the people who did this horrible thing."

Ken's demeanor had changed. He had turned his focus from Dan to the "bad guys."

The Killers and Speculation

It really hadn't occurred to me in the brief time I had known Ken, but maybe it should have. Ken was the closest to the crime, at least physically, and maybe his need for answers and justice was just as pressing as that of Dan's own friends and family. Honestly, though, there was nothing Ken could do to help solve this now ancient crime and such a quest would surely prove futile.

"I'm not sure you could, Ken," I said. "I don't know where you would start, and you would hit a wall almost immediately. I get your rage, and it's a noble thought, but I don't think you could find them. The police aren't likely to release what little evidence they have to me, much less to someone else. Honestly, Ken, I don't think they have any evidence that would hold up in a court of law today."

From our research, I had learned that during the investigation, law enforcement in California had gathered a fair amount of evidence from Dan's crime scene. They also recovered evidence from where the suspects had gotten stuck near Lavic Road in 1974. Shotgun shells, cigarette butts, I don't know what else. Evidence recovered from another, possibly related murder, might also have provided clues. I also suspected, after our visit a month earlier, that the evidence had been lost in a warehouse somewhere and most likely would never turn up. Or maybe no one was willing to expend effort on a case so old it likely can never be closed.

Ken and I shared similar feelings over this incident. The stages of grief, right? Anger is right up there near the top in most cases. Early on, I carried a great degree of anger, like many in Dan's life. Especially my father. I know he considered, probably not too seriously, getting a van, parking it in the Mojave, and lying in wait for the same guys to magically show up. He planned to lie awake fully armed with a 12-gauge shotgun. At fifteen, even I recognized the futility in such a plan. But that's what anger, or should I say rage, can do to someone. I watched the anger stage and then the depression stage take my dad. I don't think there was ever an acceptance stage. I decided I wouldn't go the same way. Such anger can tear you up if you hold it too long. Better to let it go.

I wanted to see these two men caught, but even if, by some miracle, their names dropped from the sky and into our laps, I didn't think there was evidence linking them to Dan's murder. They would have to provide a confession to solve this mystery after all this time. I could only hope.

I tried to tell Ken my rationalization regarding the murderers that has guided me for many years. Ken knew the facts. His seat was right there.

Any human being who could park on the side of the road, whip out a shotgun, walk a few feet, shoot a perfect stranger with intent to kill while that person was sleeping? Maybe grab a small sum of money then get back in a vehicle and drive away? They were awful, evil people. My mind told me they continued their evil and were either dead or in prison. Perhaps that was my justification for not following up after my father died, but I feel it to be true. This wasn't the first or the last crime Sam and the other guy committed. Maybe they did the world a favor and shot each other in a drugged-up, boozed-up rage. Darwin's theory would have played out, and the world would be a better place.

If by some miracle the killers were found, and the evidence linking them to Dan's murder was irrefutable, and the system was unable to bring them to justice, I knew of folks who gladly volunteered to fix any dangling ends. Maybe I'm one of them. I said Ken should feel free to jump on board should such an opportunity arise.

Ken grinned and nodded. "I might dust off some family heirlooms and hitch a ride with you if that ever happens."

I nodded and finished my thought. "I would rather see you spending the rest of your days in the pursuit of happiness than chasing down these creeps who likely can't be found or are permanently gone from this earth. I declared them dead and gone in my mind a long time ago."

Ken interjected, "Y'all found me."

Loretta and I laughed. "That turned out to be easy, Ken," Loretta said.

"All we had to do was ask. If we had known that we would've asked long before now."

Ken smiled and said, "That's why I was so emotional when we first talked on the phone a month ago. I've been waitin' to tell somebody somethin', somebody who cared, for all these years. Your brother saved my life. If I sound overly dramatic, I'm sorry, but I really believe that Dan saved my life. It may have been by accident or divine intervention, but your brother was my guardian angel that night and maybe has been ever since."

Ken was quiet for a few moments. Things had grown still in the pool table room, as well. I suspected the boys were taking a break from their game. I could hear the low hum of voices behind me.

Ken drew a deep breath and resumed. "Man, Dan had to have seen my big smile when I jumped into his van. I said, 'Man, thank ya, thank ya, thank ya, thank ya! Thank you, man!'

"Dan stuck out his hand and said, 'Hi, I'm Dan Walker.' He gave me a nice firm handshake."

That detail, that one detail, is something my father should have heard as painful as it may have been. Danny had pursued his own path, but he had never forgotten from where he had come and the lessons he had learned. Although taking a different path from the one preferred by my parents, that didn't make him less proud of who he was. Quite the opposite.

Ken said he and Dan hit it off right away. There was not that tense moment you often have when you first get into a stranger's vehicle. For Ken, it was a total relief. Not only had he been picked up quickly from a lonely spot on the highway, but he and Dan connected immediately, on every level.

"We were talkin' just like I'd talk to my buddies back in Texas. It was like we had known each other forever."

Ken rubbed his chin.

"It wasn't very long, Dan says, 'I'm glad I picked you up. I really would like to have the company.' He said he was on his way to Denver, so I asked him if I could just ride up to Denver with him. By then, I could maybe call home, maybe get some money, or continue hitchhiking. Anything to get me out of California and out of that desert. I felt safe with Dan. I just wanted to stay with him. He was cool."

Loretta asked, "So by the time you met Dan, he was the most normal person you had met hitchhiking?"

Ken nodded. "Yeah! Without any doubt, by far. He was certainly the most laid back. Knowin' what I know now, and, if this bad thing hadn't happened, I probably would've gone up to Denver with Dan, probably gone to work with him, and stayed in Denver for a while. Who knows? I had no ties anywhere. At that moment, I just wanted out of California. I wish Dan hadn't stopped to sleep. I believe the turns in my life would have been much different had he just said, 'You drive while I get some rest.'"

I, surprisingly, had never thought about that before. Why hadn't Dan let Ken drive? I bet during their conversation, Dan realized that Ken had been hitching all day and was probably just as tired as he was and that they both needed some sleep. It was likely going to be just a few hours' rest, and he'd be heeding Uncle Bob's advice to pull over if he got tired.

"Another question, Ken," asked Loretta.

"Detective Myler and the news back in the day said Dan picked you up near Cajon Pass. Do you know what time it was when Danny picked you up?"

"Cajon Pass?" Ken scrunched his eyebrows. "You mentioned that name, that place before. I honestly had no clue where I was when Dan picked me up, but I think it was probably around midnight or something like that."

"You think it was that late?" I asked.

"I don't know, I don't know for sure. As I said before, it was after dark. I have no idea. I wasn't wearing a watch. It could have been earlier, nine or ten, maybe. I had lost all track of time, especially after the sun went down."

Loretta nodded. "That fits a little better with the timeline we put together. The Bulls said Danny left their house around 7 p.m."

I agreed. "That timeline makes sense and matches the hours of critical note we already know."

Ken looked at us.

"In one of the pieces of information you sent, it says Dan and I went to a restaurant after Dan picked me up. Ya know, I barely remember any of those details these days. It makes sense, though. The only nourishment I had were those Budweiser tall boys during my first ride in that Opel Cadet. For all I know, I begged Dan to stop and get something to eat. Also, probably, pushed out of my brain. But years later, I was on a job in California. We went to a restaurant, and I felt like I'd been there before. I'm sure it wasn't the same place. I don't know how it could've been. But man, it felt like it. It was probably just being in California again for the first time since my ride with Dan."

"We think we found the restaurant you and Dan ate at after he picked you up," Loretta added. "It was likely something you told the cops back then being fresh in your mind. I don't know how they would have known you had stopped unless you had told them. The restaurant, we think, was in Victorville. We think it was a Denny's back in '74. It's now called Franky's. It is right off Interstate 15, old route 66. We had a late lunch there when we were doing our California research."

Ken was shaking his head.

"This is all so weird," he said. "I just haven't talked about this with anybody at all. A guy I go to church with—we used to pound one beer after another back in the day—I mentioned it to him the other day. I coulda swore I had told him years ago. He didn't know about it. I said, 'Randy, I never said anything to you about what happened?' He says, 'No, first I'm hearing about it.' I think I've been tellin' this story in my head for so long, I thought I told more people what happened way back then."

Ken smiled sheepishly. "I guess I did keep pretty quiet about it, didn't I?"

"How do you tell the story, when you do tell it, like to your buddy Randy?" I asked. "You told the story to Randy and the girl you went out with last night."

"Well, I tell it like I'm tellin' y'all. I helped this guy take a truck out to California. I was living on chips and Baby Ruth bars. I was starving and I needed to get home. The same deal, basically the same way I'm talkin' to y'all. I don't go into details or anything. It's helped me thinkin' about it and talkin' about it over the last month. I didn't realize how much in the back of my mind it was, but it's always there. I was sharing some of this with my daughter the other night, not sharing details, a father would want to skip most of what happened while sharing this story with his kids. I told her, 'You see why I worry so much? Be careful, be careful,' I said. 'Because it can all change.' Ken snapped his fingers. 'That quick!'"

I'm sure Dan and Ken went to sleep that night feeling the world was right. Dan was on the road again, a happy place for him, most likely already missing his Tustin family but on his way to see close friends in Denver, then maybe home to Illinois. Whether Ken stuck with Dan to Denver or continued toward Texas when Dan turned north, he was headed in the right direction and in good company. Both were close to realizing their immediate goal, getting out of California. They were just a little over an hour's drive from the Arizona state line when they stopped that night.

To hear that Ken felt the same way I do, that life can turn on a dime, felt good to me. It felt even better to hear him say it. I disagreed, however, with the worrying element. I wasn't a parent, though, so my outlook was likely different.

What happened to Dan is the one thing that taught me *not* to worry. It was so out of the ordinary and unexpected, one would never fret about such things. That was my takeaway from what happened to Dan. I pushed my luck, awfully hard a few times but it was the good twists of fate and not the bad ones that had befallen me. From what I knew of Ken so far, the gentle hands of fate had held him for most of his life.

"So you don't really remember stopping with Dan at the restaurant?" I reiterated. "Do you recall Dan changing his route at all? Perhaps to help you out and get you closer to Texas? The news articles at the time said he altered his route to accommodate your need to get back home because your mother was in the hospital. We're pretty sure Dan was headed to Denver where he'd lived and had friends. But if you were headed straight for Denver, Interstate 40 out of Southern California wouldn't be the most optimal route."

Ken thought for a moment.

"You know, I read that in some of those old news articles y'all sent last week. That was the first time I had heard any of that. Really! I haven't had much time to process what you sent. Hell, I'm barely processing the last few hours," Ken said with a laugh. "What happened to Dan was probably reported on in your neck of the woods where Dan was from and in the Mojave area where the murder happened and where they were searching for the killers. But it wasn't news here. Nothin'! It was like it never happened once I got off that truck at the Abilene truck stop. So no, I really don't remember it that way. I don't remember Dan and I talkin' about taking a different route. Maybe we did! We could've, but I think that would be something I would remember, something that would make me feel more guilt. I may have told him my mom was in the hospital, but I don't remember that part of our conversation. He sure as hell knew my destination was Texas."

Ken paused again.

"The news about my mom and that Dan changed his route because my mom was in the hospital? That's just not how I remember it. I didn't know my mom was feelin' bad before I left with Tommy for California. My mom's one of those people who doesn't whine—she doesn't want people to worry. I did find out she was goin' into the hospital while I was with Tommy at the Air Force base. My brother probably told me, but I didn't feel a great sense of urgency to get back. Other family members were there to pitch in and support our mom and look after Rhonda.

"I wasn't the navigator, and I didn't drive at all that night. Dan may have changed his route, but he didn't share that information with me. I don't remember us talkin' about our mother's illnesses. My main memory was us talkin' about going to Denver. Me hightailing it home wouldn't have helped my mom. Probably the best thing for me to do was stay out of the picture. Denver with Dan was on my mind."

I felt the need to interrupt, so I butted in. Ken had mentioned shouldering guilt.

"Guilt Ken? What guilt?"

Ken looked at the ground.

"I don't know, survivor's guilt? PTSD or some version of it?" Ken laughed uncomfortably.

It was something I had wondered about regarding Ken, especially recently. Ken got even more animated.

"In the last month, ever since we've been in contact," he began, "since I was able to read a few things and bring back these memories, I keep asking myself, 'Why am I alive? My God! Why am I alive?' It just doesn't make sense. Why didn't they look in back? That is why I have always thought Dan knew the guys that killed him. They never bothered to look in the back. They must have known Dan was traveling alone. The way Dan pleaded with them, the way he begged them, it was as if he knew them. If it was a robbery, why didn't that back door fly open or why didn't they break the windows? There was some valuable stuff in the back. I was in back. Yet they hardly peeked in the window. Why was I spared? Dan knew these guys. They were after him and him alone. I can come up with no other conclusion other than … Dan knew them and they were out to get Dan and nothing else."

Ken's emotional needle had turned to the negative again. Ken never had any release for all those years and had never heard any other theories. I had worried that we would cause more harm than good while pursuing this story, our little project, especially as it related to Ken now that we had found him.

The assertion that Dan knew his killers made my stomach churn, and I think Ken could tell. It was hard to hide my expression. I've never considered that a possibility, even a little. First, post investigation, that theory had been all but ruled out quickly by the detectives. It was flat-out not what they believed. Second, who would have had a grudge so serious they needed to kill Dan? He wasn't the kind of fellow prone to pissing people off. He was a mellow, laid-back guy. Dan wasn't an aggressive person who made enemies.

Dan was working two jobs during that summer. His primary job was a carpenter in a boatyard. He also had a part-time job in the evenings at a grocery store. He had just bought a VW van with his hard-earned money to move all his stuff—a small motorcycle and other personal items.

By the time he had purchased his 1957 Volkswagen bus, moving on from California was on his mind—he had stated as much in a letter home. When did he have time to make an enemy? Was it in the produce section at his part-time job? Dan and David hadn't spent every moment together that summer. David worked in one shipyard and Dan at another called Westsail, where he was, apparently well-liked. His nickname there was "Colorado."

Martha had been back from working in Utah by midsummer. She, David, and Danny spent time together when they weren't working. Martha insisted there were no "seedy" characters hanging around the house or hanging around Danny, laughing about Dan smelling of celery whenever he returned from his part-time grocery produce job.

"When Danny wasn't working, he was helping out my mom or hanging with us when we were off work with free time," Martha had said during our interview. "Dan was always pitching in with chores around the house."

What about a drug deal gone wrong in the desert? Not a likely theory, either. Dan didn't have the means to be any kind of dealer. When he was shot he had about $80 in cash in his front pants pocket and $800 in travelers checks stored in his gear. The experimental drug usage of his college days had run its course. Smoking pot was still something Dan was keen on, but a small amount of personal use marijuana, most of the time, wouldn't get you killed.

The police had interviewed David immediately and intensely in the days following Dan's murder. He reiterated to detectives that he and Dan were minor recreational marijuana users. He resented the focus he was under from the detectives, and how much time they were spending in Orange County interrogating the Bulls. David gave up every contact who he had bought even a joint from so the cops could finish their investigations in Orange County and start directing their focus back east toward the desert.

There was also speculation that Dan had stolen somebody's girl back in Denver. So … after Dan had been gone from Colorado for over two months, this unknown boyfriend drove down from Denver, randomly scoured the Mojave to find Dan, and shot him? I'd never given any credence to that theory.

The killers were only there long enough to shoot Dan, reach in for anything visibly valuable, and leave. According to reports, what was visible was pocket money Dan had in his front pants pocket that had been exposed by the shotgun blasts, as well as the keys to the van in the ignition.

I was convinced the killers didn't know Dan. They chose him at random, maybe an initiation killing with robbery as an opportunistic afterthought.

"Ken, the evidence just doesn't point to Dan knowing the guys who shot him," I said. "I have wondered, as you have, why they didn't look in the back in search of more booty. If the murderers knew Dan, were they randomly scouting Interstate 40 in hopes of running into him? Now, I get that these guys were likely not the brightest bulbs in the box, but that wouldn't have been a well-thought-out strategy. Dan barely knew he was leaving Tustin when he did, and his destination was undecided right up until the last minute. He mentioned the possibly of heading to Northern California, south to Mexico, to Denver, or maybe a straight shot home to Illinois. He could have just as easily ended up on Interstate 15 north of Barstow instead of Interstate 40 east to Needles."

Martha Bull had said, "Dan was moving on—he felt like his time was up in California. When we were shopping together for his trip, he told me about five different routes he was thinking about taking. Maybe up to Utah to see Menzies, maybe straight to Colorado, possibly back to Illinois. Anybody who thought that they knew his route … I don't think Dan knew his route as he was leaving."

I agreed with Martha's sentiments. Dan liked it that way at that time in his life. He rarely made concrete plans. Leave when leaving feels right—go the direction the road takes you. If someone had a personal score to settle with Dan, they would've had to be getting hourly updates of his ever-changing travel plans.

There was still the occasional crackling of pool balls behind Loretta and me, but it seemed like more conversation than pool playing was taking place back in the house.

Ken steered us in another direction.

"Here's a question I've wanted to know. I only knew Dan for a short time. Like I said, we hit it off immediately. There are things that are engrained in my memory. The way he introduced himself for sure, the cool relaxed way we got along." Ken hesitated. "The thing I was afraid to tell ya earlier and that I really don't want passed on, well … "

Ken looked at Loretta.

"Would ya turn off the recorder?" he asked.

Daniel My Brother Redux

"Absolutely!" Loretta said and clicked off the recorder.

"That night with Dan, we smoked some weed after he picked me up." Ken grinned guiltily. "Please, please don't repeat any of this information. I was eighteen, and eighteen was a long time ago."

Ken looked at me intently for my commitment of silence. I gave him the scouts honor sign and said, "No one hears anything from me that you do not approve of first."

Ken nodded.

We both turned to Loretta for her commitment.

"Nothing for me to tell here, guys," she said, smiling. "This isn't my story. I'm just here to participate as a facilitator and observer. You have my word of honor, but you needn't worry about me passing anything on."

So, Ken proceeded, confident that we weren't going to out his highly criminal marijuana usage with my brother thirty-six years ago while crossing the Mojave Desert in the dead of night.

"Dan and I both had some weed," Ken admitted.

"I had some 'Tops' rolling papers and a small amount of weed in a Skoal chewing tobacco tin, but Dan had a joint already rolled. He whipped it out, and we smoked a half a joint together. We got real talkative and philosophical after that. Probably hungry, too. As you said, the report says we stopped for somethin' to eat. But that was a long time ago, and I'd been on a two-week travelin' marathon.

"I'm surprised I remember as much as I do. I was wired and tired when Dan and I were talkin', not to mention stoned. Gosh, if I have it right, we spent about four or five hours gettin' to know each other. I wish I remembered more of the stuff we talked about. His first words and his last words have stayed with me forever, but there was so much more we talked about that night. Again, I felt so comfortable with him that I was considering goin' with him to Denver. That's not somethin' you make up thirty-six years later. It was definitely somethin' I had considered that night."

Ken paused again, scraping his boot soles in the dirt.

"My question is, 'Who was Dan?' He sure left an impression on me. The guy who picked me up that night is a superhero in my mind. Was he a good man?"

I was uneasy about how Ken had praised Dan over the last month since connecting. Of course, it also felt good to hear Ken speak of my brother that way.

"Do you mind if we turn the recorder back on?" I asked.

Ken nodded yes. "Oh, yeah! I'm done sharing any questionable things. That's it!"

Ken's question was likely something he'd wondered for years. Just who was this guy he rode with for hours before he witnessed his murder? There wasn't a quick-and-easy answer to Ken's question.

One consistent observation in our interviews was that Dan was "trying to find himself." A common phrase of the times aimed at deflecting parental criticism, the long form interpretation being: "Leave me alone. I will make my own way in life, and who knows? You may become proud of me. I won't be a burden. Just be patient and give me time to explore life without expectations."

Was it just me or had Dan, in his short life, had the effect on others that he'd had on me? I was his younger brother, so naturally I looked up to him. Two of Dan's friends had named sons after Dan. Another (Tom Wiznerowitz and his wife, Mary Ann) had named a daughter after Dan, Dana, who perished at birth and was buried not far from Dan. A role model of Dan's titled a book, published long after Dan's death, after a phrase Dan cited in the late-1960s as a teenager.

In ways, I barely remembered who my older brother was, and we grew up together. I certainly didn't know Dan in the ways those friends who honored him knew him.

"Was Dan a good man? I don't know," I said. "I would argue that his good traits far outweighed any bad. To use a phrase my father used in his last letter to Dan the summer of 1974, 'Everyone speaks so highly of you, always and without exception.' The same could be said for the interviews we've conducted over the last year." I paused.

"It's not easy to answer your question. I'm too close to be objective. I'm biased. He was my older brother and to my recollection, as cool, kind, and real as anyone I've ever known."

My sister would likely deflect the question as well. We two have always maintained that, of course, "Only the good die young." If they had lived, however, their goodness might have worn thin. Only those closest to Dan knew the truth. I have only heard my sister say it once, and it was said through tears. "Danny was the best of us all."

I've never prodded her further, but I think she meant that Dan had a good moral compass and a firm grasp on what was important in life. The "of us all" my sister spoke about were those he grew up with and who had influenced him. He only lived until almost twenty-two, so he was the best of all of us he knew. Our parents, my sister, the Bulls, every one of them. I can't speak for his friends, but I'm sure they wouldn't veer far from that sentiment.

"Ken, the time we've spent with Dan's friends over the last year has been pretty informative. They all spoke highly of Dan, everyone did. Rick, one of Dan's roommates in college, described Dan something like this: 'Dan was out to save the world. What I remember most about Dan was that he was the nicest guy. He was absolutely, the nicest guy. No agendas, no B.S., just the nicest guy.'"

Leslie Bull had this to say: "By age fourteen, I knew I was the complete misfit of the family. Danny never made me feel strange at any time. My own siblings, back in those teenage years, made me feel like a fish out of water in my own home. But when Dan was around us over the years and with us that summer in California, I never felt that vibe from him. He was always so warm and wonderful to me. Dan never treated me like a weirdo because my interests were different."

I continued, "One of Dan's closest friends growing up, Bob Schneider, described Dan as having 'a high cool factor, a very high cool factor.' Which made me laugh because, truly, that's the way I remembered him.

"Bob also said, 'He was adventurous and a big dreamer. He knew how to ride motorcycles and loved hot cars. He had a big circle of friends—he was good-looking and very social. Everybody liked Danny. He was a great guy who related to a lot of different people. He was also a chick magnet.'

"Bob is the friend, still alive, who I believe was closest to Dan. For a time after high school, Bob ran a handyman business over the summer and asked Dan if he could step in on a job because he was overloaded with business. Dan ended up having a Mrs. Robinson encounter from *The Graduate* for three days as one woman's personal handyman. Koo koo ka chew!"

We all laughed. I had been chuckling to myself about that one for more than a month.

Ken was still listening, but I needed another break. I was ready for more about that fateful night he'd hitched a ride with my brother.

"Ken, could I switch back to you and Dan that night? A detail that hasn't been clear to me over the years. I can't remember if I read it somewhere or if I just assumed it for some reason. Something in either a police report or a news article said you were already in the back of the VW when you guys pulled off the highway to get some sleep?"

Ken shook his head.

"No! That's not true at all. It's another fact the news media, if it was reported that way, got wrong."

"I get it, Ken," I agreed. "The media walks a fine line with me, too."

I had harbored a negative opinion over the years of the way some media outlets had reported Dan's story. A close friend who spent years in the newspaper business once told me, "Journalism is literature in a hurry." It's a quote from Matthew Arnold, an English poet from the 1800s. Journalism is most definitely that: Reporters hustling for a story and meeting a deadline, not always a perfectly precise business.

"So, you weren't in back when Dan pulled over?" I asked.

Ken shook his head again. "No, that's what I've been tryin' to tell you for the last month. We were both sittin' in the front bench seat of the van when Dan decided to pull over. It was dark. I had no idea where we were. I just knew we were goin' east on Interstate 40. Dan pulled over, maneuvered the van over a bumpy area, and backed up against a hill. He says, 'We're going to get some sleep here for a while.'"

I was glad we visited that spot. I could clearly visualize the hill.

"If you know or don't know," Ken said, "Dan had built a nice little sleeping spot behind the driver's seat. It was right in the center behind the bench seat. His motorcycle was toward the back of the van with a bunch of other stuff. The bedroll had some cushion, and he had a couple of blankets for warmth."

I said, "I don't think I knew that, Ken, or else I've forgotten any details about a bedroll. That's a new detail to me. All I ever knew is that you were in the back."

Ken nodded.

"So we stopped on the side of the road, and Dan says, 'Go ahead and get in back and get some sleep.' That's when I said, 'You let me sleep in the front here. You've got this nice comfortable bedroll all set up. You go ahead and take it.'"

Ken paused. "I'm probably repeating this to you word for word," he said. "I told Dan, 'You don't need to worry about me, I'm not goin' to try anything bad. I'm not gonna hurt you or anything. My gosh, you saved me by pickin' me up. I know you don't know me, but you can trust me. What I want is for you to do what is best for you and makes you the most comfortable. You're doin' all the driving. You need the best rest.'"

Ken paused again, longer this time, slowly shaking his head.

"That's why I remember his last words so clearly. Dan said, 'No, go ahead, take the bedroll. I'm just going to sit up here and catch the sunrise.'

"I pulled my bowling ball bag and paper bag of clothes off the passenger seat floorboard and put them in back. Then I climbed over the bench seat onto Dan's bedroll and soon I was sleeping in the comfiest spot I'd been in for weeks, maybe tied with Tommy's Silverado."

Ken mulled over his next words.

"If Dan had taken his bedroll for himself, I'd be dead, and he'd be alive."

It was just now hitting me. Oh, my God! I hadn't understood the context of the last words Dan had spoken to him until this moment. Had I never met Ken, I'd never have known of my brother's last kindhearted act.

"For whatever reason, Dan wanted the front seat. His choice meant the end of his life, and, for some unknown reason, I have no idea why, I lived through it. Dan's call was my salvation. He literally took a bullet for me. Perhaps it was accidental, but that's the way I see it. It upsets me every time I think about it, how close it came to being me. In my view, it was the second time Dan saved my life that night. First when he picked up a frightened eighteen-year-old kid at night in the Mojave Desert, and second when he insisted that I take his bedroll."

Ken looked down, scuffed his boot soles over the dirt, then looked at us, "I think about this often, you two. I'm a grandfather. Every time I babysit my grandkids, I think of Dan and I realize what an impact that one decision has made in my world. If Dan takes his own bedroll, none of what I know today exists."

I held back a bucket full of feelings over this last revelation when Ken looked toward the house and around the property and drew a deep breath.

"What do ya say? Wanna take another ride? Maybe head to Abuelo's for a late lunch?"

"Sure," Loretta and I agreed in unison.

We were on the move again. Loretta shut down the recorder.

Why So Long

We walked back into the pool table room and chatted with Derrel and the boys. We then said our goodbyes, and Derrel escorted us back through his home to his front door. We hadn't gotten to know Derrel, but he seemed like an amiable fellow. Ken and I jumped into the front seat of Ken's pickup, Loretta in the back managing the recorder.

Ken backed up and we slowly made our way to the end of Derrel's tree-canopied driveway where he stopped the truck.

"Do you mind if we skip Abuelo's for now?" Ken asked. "If we are still at it later, we can still go up to Abuelo's for a late supper or appetizer. I need to take you back there anyway to get your car. Let's hit THE SHACK where we were parked earlier. Do you mind?"

"Don't mind at all. That's fine," I spoke for Loretta, knowing that we are both barbecue fans. "Show us whatcha got in Buffalo Gap."

Ken laughed, nodded, and looked at his dashboard. It was approaching 4:00.

"They have great Texas barbecue, and it will be pretty quiet this time a day. Abuelo's back in Abilene, maybe not so much on a Saturday afternoon."

We turned left onto highway 89 and headed back toward Buffalo Gap. Ken had his right hand on the wheel, his opposite elbow on the armrest again. He shifted position to address me more directly while he drove.

"Don't be mad at me for asking this, don't hit me or anything, but, ah … why did it take thirty-six years for someone to get in touch with me or try to contact me?"

Ken asked a poignant and important question, one that had lodged itself in the back of my mind for years, even more so recently. Every time I had read news reports and articles from late-1974 or just thought about it over the years, the unasked question had jumped out at me. Doesn't anyone want to talk with "the hitchhiker" whose real name was never disclosed in any of the police reports, private investigator updates, or newspaper articles? Why had it taken so long for someone from Dan's family to contact him? One would think if Dan had a loving family, which he did, someone would have contacted Ken to find out anything more that he could tell them.

But until a month ago, until now, I wasn't sure that no one had.

"Ken," I started, "I doubt I can give you a clear answer that will sit well with you. I'm sorry. I don't blame anyone, nor should anyone shoulder any guilt. I suppose it was for many reasons it happened that way. First and foremost, I believe, the police had advised that we not contact the hitchhiker. 'He doesn't know anything—he can't tell you any more than he has told us to help the investigation. He was a frightened young man who was in the wrong place at the wrong time.'"

Ken nodded as he drove.

It was true, as far as I knew. My father took law enforcement's advice and left Ken alone. The police had assured him they had fully cleared Ken and there was no reason to contact him. It may only traumatize the hitchhiker further. I honestly didn't believe my father knew Ken's name. If he did, he never told us. Also, he may have thought that meeting and talking with Ken would only have caused him more pain. In addition to the cops saying don't bother the young hitchhiker, I'm not sure my father had it in him to meet Ken and hear his story. He was barely holding it together after Dan's murder.

We had also recently interviewed Bob Bull, and we asked him if there had been any attempt to contact Ken back in the seventies. He and my dad had worked hand-in-hand with the police. Uncle Bob Bull was my father's boots on the ground in California, and there was nothing my father's good friend wouldn't do for him or for the son that he, too, had lost. He was the first family representative to get to Needles the day Dan was shot. It fell to Uncle Bob to identify Dan's body. He told me he hadn't contacted the hitchhiker for the same reason—because the police had told him there was no reason to do so. The hitchhiker could add nothing further to help solve the case.

We were coming into Buffalo Gap when I remembered something important that might address Ken's earlier expressed lingering guilt.

"Like I said earlier, Ken, in between finding out your name and coming down to see you, we were able to spend some time with my Uncle Bob. He's eighty-two now. We have about two hours of him on tape. I don't remember all the details of our discussion, but I do remember this, and I think it's something you would like to hear."

The cops were confident, convinced Ken had been perfectly cooperative, and they imparted that to Uncle Bob. There was never any question, in their view, that Ken had done the right thing at every turn that morning. The police believe nothing Ken could have done would have changed what happened and that Ken's cooperation was 100 percent sincere in law enforcement's view.

As to involving the media, Uncle Bob thought that the hitchhiker and his "heroics" that morning should be included in the news flashes to garner further interest and attention to the case. But it was either nixed by the police or by the media for whatever reason. Maybe the police were trying to protect Ken? The murderers were still at large, and Ken was the only eyewitness.

"Ken," I started, "Uncle Bob told the investigators to extend every appreciation to you, from both him and my father, for all you tried to do for Dan that morning. They feared you would have survivor's guilt and wanted to tell you that they believe you acted bravely that morning in all that you did for Dan."

We pulled into THE SHACK lot. Ken shifted his truck into park and turned away. He was quiet, looking out the driver's side window.

"I'm racked with a lot of emotion right now. Hang on."

Ken took a moment to compose himself.

"That never made it to me," he said. "That means more to me than I can tell you. I have always thought the opposite about myself and my actions that morning, thinking I should've done more for Dan."

There was nothing more Ken could've done. He couldn't have stopped Dan from dying. By the time he knew there was trouble afoot, my guess was Dan was already beyond saving. Ken wasn't armed. Him jumping out of the back of the van would only have gotten him killed, too.

Ken, composed now, listened as I continued.

"It should also be said that everyone was concentrating their efforts, physical and emotional, on getting justice for Dan. Dan's death destroyed my father in ways that aren't easy to describe and you likely wouldn't care to hear about. Even though he and Dan had some differences, the love and respect between them ran deep. My father was devastated. He blamed himself for what happened. I think my mother blamed him, as well. I never heard her express it out loud, but I suspected behind closed doors, after a few drinks, she made her opinion known."

"They worked hard with the cops on the investigation?" Ken asked.

"Oh my God, Ken, yes!" I said.

I explained that I had little doubt that Dan's case was pursued by our family and Uncle Bob until the leads went cold and the emotional tank ran dry. I was fifteen at the time, going on sixteen through the investigation. My father wasn't sharing information directly with me, but it was impossible not to know what was going on around you under the same roof. Plus, there was substantial documentation from that year. My father was a letter writer, a pretty good one, too. I think every moment he wasn't tending to work and family, he was pursuing leads and writing letters.

My father and Uncle Bob followed the investigation closely. Uncle Bob offered a substantial reward to anyone who could provide information leading to the van or the suspects. My father and his friend followed up with the detectives often and used whatever pull they had in their industry to spread the word and develop leads. Uncle Bob was an executive officer at CBS, working for their musical instrument division that included Fender guitars, Rogers drums, and Rhodes pianos. He held that position from 1972 to 1977, and he used his connections to the media to get the word out about the gold van and as much information about the suspects as they could fit into the various ad spaces. Uncle Bob went on television in California to publicize the case further. His identity was hidden in some fashion because they still had no motivation for Dan's murder. It could've been a corporate grievance "weirdo" scenario. Since Dan had been living with the Bulls, maximum precaution was being taken. Uncle Bob wanted to include Ken's actions that morning to spur more interest and publicity, but somewhere along the chain, that idea was nixed.

"Really?" Ken responded. "I wish they had. I wish someone would've called me to ask."

Not long after detectives put Ken on the truck back to Abilene and Dan was buried, my father flew to California with my sister to meet and speak with the detectives about the case and take care of other details. They stayed overnight at the Bull's place in Tustin, and Uncle Bob drove them up to San Bernardino to meet with the team investigating the crime.

My father wrote letters to different states, different government agencies, pushing and trying to help the investigation in any way he could. He targeted Indiana in particular, contacting the department of education for leads on any kids in the school system whose father had the first name of Sam.

I then remembered something else I believed Ken would want to know.

Another fact that surely never reached Ken in Texas. It was kind of new to me. Let's call it a renew because I remembered some of it from way back. Investigation and research brought the memory back.

Six days after Dan was shot, on October 7, 1974, someone murdered a highway maintenance worker driving a state garbage truck. It was eerily like what happened to Ken and Dan. It happened off Interstate 8 near Casa Grande, Arizona, at a rest stop. That was about 400 miles from where Ken and Dan had parked in the Mojave.

Ken stared wide-eyed at me as I shared this forgotten fact. I closed my eyes and shook my head in disgust.

This Arizona highway worker was shot in the upper torso and face. His billfold was gone. He had just emptied a trash can and was putting in a new liner. It also happened very early in the morning. There were no witnesses. A truck driver who came upon the scene around 8:30 that morning discovered him.

I paused, remembering the news article from 1974, recently mined from the Internet.

The victim was a local guy from Picacho, Arizona. His name was Tommy Hanna. He was in his forties. Tommy had been with the Arizona Highway Department for twenty-three years. He was married with two daughters. A guy out doing his job, trying to make a living. They think the murderers got away with between $5 and $7 dollars from Tommy's wallet.

"Did they catch the guys who killed this Tommy?" Ken asked.

I shook my head.

Tommy Hanna's murder was like what happened to Ken and Dan. Secluded place, early in the morning, shotgun blasts to the upper torso and head. No witnesses at all this time. If Ken had not been there with Dan and got his rough description into the hands of the authorities, they likely wouldn't have been able to track them to the beer truck driver or the waitresses. They would have had nothing if Ken hadn't been in the back of Dan's van that morning. Tommy Hanna had nothing in the way of a witness. They found Tommy Hanna's wallet a little more than a year later in a ditch south of Tucson, near a town called Dragoon. Everything was intact except for the cash. Investigators were unable to extract any new evidence from the wallet. It was semi-significant, though, since Dragoon is east of where Tommy Hanna was killed. If the guys who killed Dan also killed Tommy Hanna, they were still heading east when they dumped Tommy's wallet. Perhaps on their way to Indiana.

Ken turned away shaking his head. There was a short lull in the conversation. A moment of silence for Tommy Hanna.

To put extra eyes on Dan's murder investigation, Uncle Bob and my father hired a private investigator to work with the police. But a year passed and nothing. No leads. The last written correspondence from the private investigator was in July 1975. He believed the police had done an "excellent" job following the case and was confident it was only a matter of time until they would catch the perpetrators.

To my mind, given this many years of hindsight, they were words intended to give some comfort to grieving relatives, even when there was little or no hope of resolution.

The investigation went to every Earl Scheib auto painting shop between California and Indiana, looking for a gold van that might have been repainted to avoid detection.

Grasping for straws, late in the investigation, my father considered consulting a famous psychic at the time, Peter Hurkos. I don't know if they ever did but that's how desperately they worked to help find the killers.

Ken said, "Wow, they went to that length?"

"Yeah, at least for that first year or two. I have read about families who make it their sole mission in life to solving their loved one's murder. I don't know why my father stopped. I think he felt a degree of futility chasing Dan's case and chose to make other aspects of his life a priority."

My father did keep searching for the "why" for a long time. Another weird, perhaps existential accident on my brother's part was a notation we found in his collection of C.S. Lewis' *Chronicles of Narnia*. In the fifth book, *A Horse and His Boy*, Dan had written inside the front cover: "Page 67." When we turned to page 67, the chapter was titled *Across The Desert*. My father read every book cover-to-cover looking for further messages or answers, but, of course, there were none.

At the time of Dan's death, my sister Debbie had just had her first child, a daughter, Sarah, in March of '74. Dan's godchild. My parents were eager and loving grandparents. They still had a fifteen-year-old in high school. My dad still had a job, and my folks still had to be the best parents they could be given the nightmare that had befallen them. I hate to say it this way, but for several reasons, they chose to move forward and stuff this tragedy. I don't know if it was the healthiest way to handle it, but that's what happened. That's how they dealt with it.

"I stuffed it, too," Ken said. "Deeply. I get what they was goin' through. I didn't handle it in a healthy way either. We likely all should've gotten therapy, but it wasn't what you did back then."

I nodded.

"As you know all too well, Ken, the world goes on, but it was a brutal time for our small family. The world went back to 'normal,' but as it probably was for you after getting back to Abilene, it was anything but normal."

Ken nodded his agreement while I explained events in our new normal.

The saddest memory for me was arriving home one evening not long after Dan's death. My father was out of town on business. My mom was, unusually, nowhere to be found. After searching the house up and down and calling a few neighbors to see if she had gone visiting, I finally checked the basement. I found my mom passed out on top of Danny's steamer trunk that had contained all his possessions. That trunk was in the van next to Ken that night. There was half a bottle of Scotch and an empty highball glass next to her and the trunk. I was unable to wake her to go upstairs to bed.

No one's routine had changed, but the spring in my parents' steps was gone. We tried to go back to a state that no longer existed. Even traditions lost their spark for a few years. My only memory of Christmas Eve 1974 was sitting on my sister's front stoop with my father in tears against my chest, begging Dan and the universe for forgiveness.

I don't have all the details, but according to her husband, my sister went into a period of darkness after October 1974. I never asked her about it until much later in life, not wanting to pick at her emotional wounds. When I finally asked, she confided that the darkness had never fully gone away. Deb and her husband had just started a family at the time of Dan's death and the subsequent investigation. There was no way she was going to dive into Dan's cold case. Even if her emotions would have allowed her to do so, it would have taken time, energy, and money to pursue the investigation. It wasn't the way she wanted to spend her future.

Debbie and her husband had another daughter in '77, adding joy to my parents' lives. In 1980, my father went to work for another piano company in North Carolina, in management this time. Not long after landing his more prestigious position, he was diagnosed with cancer, pretty much everywhere in his body. In March 1983, he succumbed to the disease at fifty-five. Cigarettes, booze, and growing up near Louisiana's cancer alley had contributed to my father's death, no doubt. But, in my view, Dan's loss and whatever personal guilt my father carried was really what took him. Even with the joy of grandchildren and a new challenging chapter in his career, the weight never lifted from his permanently weakened shoulders.

I don't think my father stayed very diligent with the detectives after the first two or three years. I wasn't keeping track. I wasn't involved, nor, at fifteen, should I have been. The odds of finding the perpetrators were next to nil. My father died four months before I graduated from college. My mom wasn't going to pick up a torch my father hadn't carried for seven-plus years. She just wanted peace, happiness, and her grandkids. She died thirteen years after her husband in her late sixties.

There was a time, when my mom was still alive and in communication with Uncle Bob, he was considering getting *Unsolved Mysteries* or *Cold Case Files* interested in Dan's case. Either he never followed through, or the shows turned it down. I don't know much about what Uncle Bob attempted, just that he mentioned it to my mom.

"It's not my nature to have done this either, Ken. Persistent urgings and encouragement from Loretta over the years, along with questions from curious nieces, made me overcome the resistance. I finally made room in my life to take on this research."

Ken nodded. "I'm really glad you did. Really glad! Let's get something to eat," he said, opening the driver's door.

Loretta shut down the recorder, and we all climbed out.

THE SHACK was a well-kept old building furnished with, not surprisingly, a Western motif. The front half was for family dining with a high counter that ran the length of one wall. In one corner sat a middle-aged man reading the newspaper. We followed Ken through the front dining area through swinging doors into the back part of the building. It was more a bar than a restaurant in back, but Ken assured us we could get food there, too. Passing a couple that looked in their fifties, we moved to the back corner and grabbed a high-top table next to the billiards table.

The music wasn't too loud. A woman about our age came to the table to greet us and get our order. She wore a wry look.

"Been awhile," she said to Ken.

Ken responded, "It sure has. How ya been, Vicki?"

"Good. Can't complain. Nobody'd listen if I did," Vicki answered. Then, arching her eyebrows, she asked, "What can I get y'all to drink?"

Both Ken and I yielded to Loretta for her choice of beverage.

"I'll go with a Miller Lite," Loretta said. "Could we get three waters too, please?"

Vicki nodded.

"I'll have a Miller High Life," I said.

Ken ordered a margarita, whereupon Vicki, wearing one of the flattest expressions I've seen in my many years of dining out, nodded, turned, and retreated toward the bar. I sensed that Ken and Vicki shared a history of some sort, small-town stuff.

"Vicki and her husband have owned this place for years," Ken said. "I've known Vicki pretty much my whole life, well, since I've been in Buffalo Gap. She is two years younger—we went to the same small elementary school together. Vicki's mom used to run this place back in the day. I think Vicki has been workin' in this building for thirty-plus years. She has seen it all in this little town. Even me in my craziest days. I haven't been here in a long time. I curbed my alcohol consumption to nearly zero, startin' back around 1999. It coincided with my last divorce and still another crazy time in my life, but it was time for me to tone it down, way down. I even went to a few AA meetings. I was a wild man when I drank. Hell, I'm kinda wild when I don't drink, so things needed to change."

I nodded and laughed. I should probably have quit drinking by now, as well, and it was beginning to look like our recent involvement with Ken had reactivated some former unhealthy habits.

"I'm still curious about Dan—what more can you tell me?" Ken asked. "It may be tedious for you, but I've wondered about these things for years. I want to know as much as you are willin' to tell me. There's no one else who can tell me the things I'd like to know, and I feel like the only people who care about this are sitting right here. It feels good being able to find all this out after years of wonderin.'"

I nodded. "It's not tedious telling *you* about Dan. I would want to know if I were you, and your interest makes it easy to talk about."

Dan's life the couple of years before he met Ken was a vibrant adventure story. I've had a great life and I've been able to travel, both for business and pleasure, but at fifty, I remain envious of my brother's adventures. I likely still haven't experienced as much of the world as Dan had in just less than twenty-two.

Europe '72

Dan's trip to Europe and beyond in fall 1972 into late-spring 1973 was an adventure in so many ways, not the least of which being his negotiations with the Selective Service during his travels. He had planned and saved for the trip since his departure from St. Norbert. It began with still more conflict on the home front.

My parents taught us the importance of personal privacy. We never rummaged through Mom's purse. We were respectful of others' property, including correspondence through the mail, diaries, and the like. However, my father broke that rule the very same hour Dan was about to leave for his trip overseas.

Bob Schneider was Dan's ride to the airport that day. After running a few last-minute errands, they had swung by our house to pick up Dan's gear before departing for O'Hare. Dan walked in the door to find his father with the opened letter addressed to my brother. It was Dan's notice to report for his preinduction physical. The Selective Service had become aware that Dan was no longer in school, and the notice had arrived at the worst possible moment. A big fight had ensued as my father insisted Dan forgo his trip and report for his physical.

Dan railed against my father for opening his mail and said, "No way! My bags are packed. They can find me in Europe if they want me that bad."

Bob Schneider recalls it being another bad scene between father and son, resulting in still more words that couldn't be taken back. There was nothing that could've stopped Dan from getting into Bob's car that day and going to the airport. My father should have known that and perhaps he shouldn't have opened Dan's mail.

Vicki came across the bar with a tray to deliver beverages.

"You gonna order something to eat, too?" she asked, putting the drinks in their correct places along with a water glass for each of us.

Ken answered for us all. "Yeah, we're gonna have somethin' to eat. Give us a bit. We may be here a while."

Vicki returned to the bar.

I raised my bottle of High Life for a toast. Loretta and Ken followed.

"Well," I awkwardly started, "here's to being here after thirty-six years."

"To Dan. Here's to Dan!" Ken upped my toast. "It's long overdue," he added.

I couldn't talk. I got choked up. I took a big gulp of my beer to shield my emotions the best I could.

"Margaritas still taste as good as they used to!" Ken said.

We were quiet, enjoying our first sips as I tried to recall all that had gone down as Dan left for his dream trip to Europe. It was another moment that had weighed on my father, words he wished he hadn't said. It also gave Bob Schneider another impression that my father was strict. He was impatient, stubborn, and a very passionate man. If viewed from the outside, one might find it to be strict-but that wasn't my view. Fact is, he also had many more positive than negative traits and was simply an imperfect man trying to be the best husband and father he could be. If Dan's life hadn't prematurely ended in a violent twist of fate, he might have felt like he had succeeded.

Dan had rolled the dice dropping out of school but not without calculated odds. By fall 1972, the war in Vietnam was winding down. Popular opinion was trending in his favor, and he negotiated his situation as a responsible adult.

Dan was a good communicator. He contacted the draft board as he was leaving that day for Europe. He explained his situation, having worked the summer at a filthy job, now embarking on a long-planned trip out of the country, tickets purchased and scheduled to depart on the very day the letter to report arrived. The draft board advised Dan to continue his trip but stay in touch during his travels.

Traveling by himself, Dan intended to meet up in Eastern Europe with his friend John O'Donnell, who would leave on a later date. Dan encountered further snags at O'Hare that made his departure even more hectic, including misplacing his camera which, he later wrote, a "long legged stewardess" returned to him.

His plane landed in Lisbon, where he started working his way through Western Europe. Dan traveled across Spain, visited Toledo, and bought a sword in the region where Quixote tilted with windmills and battled traders who insulted his love, Dulcinea. That sword adorned the mantle of our fireplace alongside Dan's harpoon from New England before also being relegated to a corner in the basement.

In France in late-November, he picked up two bayonets, relics from World War One. After France, Dan went south to Milan, Florence, Rome, and the Amalfi Coast, traveling cheaply, making friends along the way.

Early December 1972

Dear Mom and Dad,

Tomorrow I leave for Greece with or without John because of Uncle Sam. John's message says if I miss him, he will be at the Athens American Express office. I only have about twenty days and if I'm not inducted by then I'll be free of the whole mess. I feel I can't afford not to get down to Greece without enough time to check out what is going on.

Florence was OK. The people dress like models from either Vogue or Playboy. I saw the Medici Chapel, Michael Angelo's David, and a bunch of other stuff. Ate a lot of good pastry, minestrone, and ice cream for which Italy is famous.

If I miss John here tomorrow I feel confident I'll see him in Greece. I'll leave a note here telling him where I've gone to. So everything is cool.

I have to water down and feed the camel.

Love, Danny

Mid-December 1972

Dear Mom and Dad,

This probably won't reach you until after Christmas. I hope you will forgive me for not writing sooner. The whole thing with Uncle Sam has been straightened out, a little. I had to write the Commander In Chief of European Armed Forces. It looks like I'll have to take my physical in Iraklio, which is a city on the northern coast of Crete. It won't be too bad because that is where I am now. I went down the eastern and southern coast of Italy & the central part of Greece. I stayed in Athens for about a week then took a boat to Crete.

During our research and after talking with various friends of Dan, mostly Jim Fitzsimmons, who traveled with John O'Donnell on his first trip across Europe, we discovered that "a boat" often equated to a low-budget freighter, sometimes transporting handcuffed criminals and other riffraff. That's how they got from Italy to northern Greece and later, it was rumored, from Crete to Turkey.

> *I now reside in a Pensione named Angelos, on the northwest coast of Crete. The sun is shining and it's about 60 degrees outside. This morning I laid on the beach for a while & caught a few rays. Besides a small olive oil factory and a small fleet of fishing boats, two, tourists are the main source of income. There is not a paved road in the town, one bar, three grocery stores, three restaurants.*
>
> *Speaking of food, there is a shish-kabob thing in Greece called souvlaki. Athens had about fifty stands (like taco stands). I hit all of these except I hit them all twice. The Greeks have also perfected a formula for rice pudding that makes it quite addicting. Chuck, Charlie, Bruce, and me (Charlie being a Charlene) went into one place. Between us we ate two souvlakis a piece, three rice puddings, one milk, and one piece of cake. Souvlaki is pretty healthy, plus salads, moussaka, and other Greek dishes. I think, believe it or not, I have gained some weight. Ouzo is a Greek liquor, about four shots wipes you out.*
>
> *Chuck, Charlie, and Bruce are all good people. Charlene and Bruce may be a little more sane at times than Chuck (Ohio) and me. Good people, all of them. From here I will go to Ierapetra on the southeast side of the island. Then to Egypt across North Africa to the Canary Islands. If John catches up to me maybe my plans will change. However, you will be able to get in touch at 5 post Restaunte, Ierapetra, Crete, Greece.*
>
> *Merry Christmas to all. Many times I feel real bad about not being able to make it. We'll have many more. Hope Mom's*

back is as strong as a bull. Good exercise would be a backpack and 20 pounds for 20 miles a day.

All my love, Danny

I have wondered at times how long Chuck, Charlie (Charlene), and Bruce, traveled with Dan. It sounds as if they became friends and traveled together for a long period while in Europe. Did they write after spending time traveling together? When those letters from Dan stopped, did they think Dan had lost interest in communicating? Did they never find out what happened to their traveling companion?

Dan had been communicating with the US Government from the time he boarded his flight at O'Hare. During those exchanges, I'm sure he made it clear that he wasn't interested. Additionally, the war was winding down, and the draft was ending.

On February 2, 1972, the government held a drawing to determine draft priority numbers for men born in 1953, but in early 1973, secretary of Defense Melvin Laird announced that no further draft orders would be issued. So-called "Vietnamization," training, equipping, and increasing the role of the Army of the Republic of Vietnam (ARVN) while drawing down American ground forces had been policy since 1969. December 1972 saw the last men conscripted born in 1952. At the end of January 1973, the Paris Peace Accords yielded a cease-fire agreement between the United States and North Vietnam. American POWs began returning home. The Selective Service assigned draft priority numbers for all men born in 1954, 1955, and 1956, in case the government extended the draft, but it never did.

"They never took him," Bob Schneider said. "The whole thing was a colossal waste of time, money, and emotion. The fights Vietnam caused between your dad and Danny never needed to happen."

Bob was right. If you took the Vietnam "conflict" out of their lives, all the other disputes between my father and Dan would have amounted to minor skirmishes.

January 9, 1973

On Christmas Eve, I was in Agia Galini, Crete. I was leaving one of the supermarkets (which much resembles the one above Uncle Nel's camp in Louisiana) munching a chocolate bar. I broke off a chunk & gave it to Charlie & then dropped the other part because I saw John. Probably one of the best Christmas Eve presents I've ever received.

Most likely we will head for Algiers & Timbuktu after our lease is up. I don't have any definite plans. I still have 21 more days in Crete.

Algiers? Timbuktu? My gosh! I didn't know if he made it to those places, but I also had no reason to believe he didn't. He was a seasoned and fearless traveler at that point. He also had John O'Donnell by his side. John had been traveling the region extensively almost since graduation. I bet he did make it to Timbuktu just to be able to say he'd been to Timbuktu. That was Dan's style.

If the two did make it to Timbuktu, they likely made it across all North Africa to Spain's Canary Islands, and I would be even more impressed. I couldn't confirm where they went or what they did. Dan wasn't home long enough for us to hear his travel stories. Debbie didn't hear them, either. We all thought we had plenty of time, over a Thanksgiving dinner perhaps or over cold beers at a bar. I'm sure Dan thought the same. If only we had started our project earlier, we could have asked John, but tragically he died in the mid-nineties, having lived a fast life.

Shortly after John and Dan returned to the states late that spring, they were off to Denver, back to the house on University Avenue.

Back To Denver

Vicki came over and checked on us with a lit cigarette between her fingers. "Y'all doin' OK?"

I ordered another beer. I wouldn't be driving for a while, and if I did need some time to sober up, Loretta could take over and get us to wherever we needed to be, always the more prudent one, rarely one to overindulge, unlike me, my family, my friends, my workmates, and everyone I grew up with through the years.

"I'll stick with water," Loretta said.

Vicki didn't offer Ken another drink. He had taken only a sip or two of his margarita.

"You ready to order something to eat?" Vicki asked.

Ken looked at us. "You guys ready? You hungry?"

Loretta laughed. "I'm always ready to eat. Let's order."

Ken led off, giving Vicki his order. Loretta and I both safely followed. "We'll have what he's having."

Over barbecue at THE SHACK, I continued telling Dan's story as his path got closer to intersecting with Ken's.

John and Dan had an epic adventure over the last months, but getting back to Denver also felt good, back to a familiar group of friends, including roommates enrolled at Regis. It was the second half of 1973. Roommates and visitors, both male and female, came and went. Dan started working as an apprentice carpenter and, in his free time, spent as much time as possible in the mountains. Having parted company with the untrustworthy MG, Dan bought a small motorcycle to get around town, to work, and into the high country. It was a used Honda CB 200. He couldn't afford much more.

The place on University was a collegiate party house packed with fun-loving young people and, of course, Dan fit right in, having studied at the feet of the finest of merrymakers, our parents. He was also resourceful.

During a weekend-long party at their place, while they roasted chickens hanging from a curtain rod spanning a bed of coals in the driveway, Dan remembered his family connections in Louisiana. Dan said, "I bet I can get us some fresh seafood flown in."

They took a collection, and they came up with about a $100. "Fitz" and John were familiar with Dan's Louisiana lineage, having attended parties back in Mundelein featuring seafood buffets flown in or brought in by visiting relatives.

Many at the weekend bash doubted Dan's grand plan of delivering a fresh seafood feast for the masses—that is until a call came in from the airport cargo terminal. They said a huge shipment of seafood had arrived from Louisiana, that it was perishable, and needed to be picked up immediately.

"How huge?" Jim Fitzsimmons remembered asking the cargo folks.

The answer: "You better bring a pickup truck."

Dan had scored five Styrofoam coolers stuffed full of fresh oysters, crab, crawfish, and shrimp.

I didn't know how much seafood $100 could buy in the seventies or how much it would cost to pack it all in dry ice and ship it from Louisiana to Denver overnight. Nor did I know which of our Louisiana relatives came through for Dan, but I had my suspicions. I suspected, whoever it was put their thumb on the scales along with extra cash to help make Dan's plan a smashing success. Jim "Fitz" remembered everyone's surprise at Dan coming through.

"It was enjoyed. It made the party and the weekend."

Denver was a great spot for a romantic dreamer like Dan. John Denver's "Rocky Mountain High" hit number nine on the Billboard US Hot 100 in 1973. While Joe Walsh mowed his lawn one day, looking up at the Front Range, and mulling over his days with the James Gang, "Rocky Mountain Way" came to him, also released in 1973. Dave Loggins' April 1974 release of the song "Please Come To Boston" romanticized Denver and may have helped fuel Dan's passion for seeking new landscapes he hadn't yet seen.

For my birthday in March 1974, two records arrived from Denver, gifts from my older, world-traveling brother. I'm sure I received other gifts that year, but those are the ones I remember. I was thrilled to start my own library of music with Seals and Crofts' *Year of Sunday* and Simon and Garfunkel's *Greatest Hits*. Little did I know I would inherit Dan's entire record collection by the end of the year. He had an eclectic taste in music: Chuck Mangione, Taj Mahal, Brian Augers Oblivion Express, The Rascals, Elton John, Dan Fogelberg, Rare Earth, Sly and the Family Stone, Earth, Wind and Fire, Crosby, Stills, Nash, and Young, The Jimmy Hendrix Experience, The Youngbloods, Leo Kotke, and the Allman Brothers. There were more—I can't remember them all.

A month later, in April, Dan returned to Illinois for a short visit and to celebrate. It was also an opportunity to test the temperature at home. We had barely laid eyes on him for more than a year. I remember it being wonderful, everyone enjoying the time together. Peace had come to our home. I remember no conflict at all. All the stupid, bad things that could have been said had been said, and the primary catalyst, Vietnam, was now moot. Debbie and Denis' first child, a daughter named Sarah Lynn

Terry, was born in late-March. Dan was her godfather. Everyone was off to Baraboo in April for the baby's christening. It was a great family-and-friends get-together.

Dan's visit home that spring ended with the family converging in Libertyville before Dan headed back to Denver.

Dan and his father scraped up the turf in the back yard. Dan laid the forms, planned the delivery, and poured a new concrete patio behind the house. Dan engraved his initials with the date in one corner. It was a cool display of father-and-son teamwork with my brother running the show and displaying his new construction know-how. We hadn't experienced that much domestic peace in a long time. The patio was perfect. The time was perfect. There were better family days ahead, I was sure.

The last family photo of Dan was taken with Sarah Lynn cuddling and fussing in his arms. Dan went back to Denver after the patio was finished. It was last time my sister and I would see our brother, and the last time my parents would see their son.

Dan holding Sarah. Our last family photo of Dan. April 1974

Please Come to L.A.

Upon returning to Denver, Dan was ready for something new. The Denver party scene was growing old, and Dan had rambling on his mind. He reached out to David Bull in California, who offered many inducements, including spending time with his other family.

May 21, 1974

Dear Dan,

Thanks for the letter. Do you realize that you haven't written me for nearly four years? I guess I haven't written you for almost that long, though, right?

Hearing from you was delightful. I'm amazed still that you and I fostered the same ambition to sail even though we never talked during that time. Knowing carpentry is an excellent skill for both constructing and voyaging. How much experience as a carpenter have you had? Boatyards are continually advertising for experienced anybodies to build yachts, etc. out here.

It sounds like you have a terrible impression of L.A. Forget it, you won't ever have to go there. I've been there several times and it didn't seem so bad. As for the vast expanse of city that emanates well beyond the L.A. city limits and the L.A. county limits, we live at the outskirts, located an hour out of L.A. in Orange County, home of John Birchers (ever hear of them?). It takes about twenty minutes to get to the beach. Orange County is located pleasantly close to the Mexican border. This part of California has been doing steady construction and home building since I've been here.

If you haven't yet decided to come on out to the Coast, I'll have to think of better means to persuade you. Anyhow, move out here! High school labor doesn't hit the streets until the middle of June, but many colleges finish in May. I get out on the 31st of May, not far off. My attempts to get a job boatbuilding have been fruitless so far. Everyplace I tried wanted someone with experience at something or other. Becoming an apprentice might be possible, but it takes four years to complete that route. I want to sail in less than four years; way less! I didn't even take shop in high school, so I don't have any skills but cooking. That might force me to take such a job this summer if all else fails.

Your friend who wants to sail sounds fine. I can round up the necessary remaining swabbies if we cannot procure a crew of sun goddesses. Now, we've got to get this project beyond the stage of intangible dreams to material progress.

You sure didn't say much about yourself, like what you've done for the last four years. I've been going to college for three years making sure I stay out of Vietnam, working toward an English and literature degree, and dabbling in some counter-culture pass times.

Unless you are making too much money (you're only conceivable excuse), make like horse shit (hit the trail) and move to California. I repeat, it will not be in L.A. The best harbor (I think) is near here in Newport, many miles South of L.A.

Presumably still?

Your friend,

Dave

P.S. Have you heard from Richard? Did you hear about the S.L.A. shootout? Symbionese Liberation Army? We watched it on TV. Martha and I went to the California Jam concert (200,000).

Rare Earth, Earth Wind and Fire, The Eagles, Seals and Crofts, Black Oak Arkansas, Black Sabbath, Deep Purple, and Emerson Lake and Palmer played at California Jam on April 6, 1974. The music scene in California and Uncle Bob's access to that scene might have also drawn Dan to take the Bulls up on their invitation. The Bull kids got great tickets and sometimes backstage passes for popular performers, but it was the possibility of sailing the seas that really hooked Dan.

David had been a sailor from his earliest days and, as kids, he and Dan had done some rudimentary sailing in a Sunfish on Sylvan Lake. Now they were thinking of building a sailboat capable of crossing oceans. There was even talk of renting a home closer to the water to make it easier to launch a craft with a concrete-hull design Dan had read about.

The book *Concrete Boatbuilding, Its Technique, and Its Future* had been in the steamer trunk Dan left behind. The idea, as I looked at the binding in my younger years, had always seemed counterintuitive. Concrete? Water? Boats? But in just reading the cover flap, I learned the process was less expensive and resulted in a fireproof hull impervious to rot, borers, or rust. Maintenance was low, repairs were easy, and the hull was self-insulating, cool in the summer, warm in the winter. David also figured they'd be protected from the likes of Jaws taking a chunk out of the hull.

The pair had big sailing yacht dreams on a skiff budget, but, if you never had dreams, they never came true.

May 23, 1974 (from Denver)

Dear Debbie & Denis,

Strawberry & Rhubarb sounds funny, tastes great. Steve & I sampled it as soon as we got home & found the package. We don't work together we just sample jam together. I'm a carpenter, he's a gardener.

I've been building houses from the ground up. I've learned tons of carpentry tricks & above all I've been missing all my fingers, which is very important when you're using a 28-ounce framing hammer. However I did hit my leg. So I'm sporting a marvelous tan from the waist up and a medium tan from the thighs down with a waffle mark on my right leg. It was a pretty square hit so I just dented the flesh and didn't rip it open. To top it all off I'm making $3.75 per/hr. I work my butt off for it though. Soon I'll be able to spit nails into a wall, hold a window in one hand & a level in the other.

Went to the mountains on my motorcycle the other day. It was fantastic. I guess they're the only reason I live here. Next I think I'd like to live on the sea, or at least near the sea.

I guess you had your first mother's day & I like the ass I am, didn't do much for it. I thought about you & sexy Sarah, that's about it. I'm a real turd for that, but I guess that's why they invented it (I mean to think of all the mothers that are around). Anyway, an official Happy Mother's Day.

I'm very tired. My arm keeps moving up down, up down. It gets used to that motion after eight hours of it. If you want me to build you a house I will (I could really do it). I can hardly see the paper anymore, much less think of something neat to write about.

Give Sexy Sadie (Sarah) a smooch, ya'll. Thanks for the jam. Sorry for being a turd.

Always Yours,

Danny

June 2, 1974

Dear Sarah,

Hi, I'm your uncle Danny. You probably don't remember me from the last time you saw me because young people are like that, although it was just a few weeks ago. You were pretty mad 'cause I had taken you away from your mother. Your mom took a picture of us together. I have real long hair (for a boy) & you have a red face (for a girl). Someday I'll show it to you.

I feel like I'm going to be pretty rich pretty soon. I'm a carpenter (a guy who builds houses with wood). I found a job that pays $5.50 per/hr (which is a lot of money for Denver, Colorado, which is where I'm living now). We work really long hours & a six-day week. Nothing I think you would like to do, except of course if you like working. The job pays $330 a week.

That's why I'm pretty rich, I think?

But I guess I'll spend it all soon on this big sailboat I'm going to build with three other people (so far). One I have known as long as, well, as long as I've been alive. Ya see your grandfather Walker and my friend's father worked together for many years.

Anyway we want to build this boat & sail around the world. Maybe we won't go that far but maybe we will. If the boat is finished when you are old enough maybe you can go too. But your mom & dad will probably say no & you will go to grammar school, which is good. Anyone who wants to go around the world should go to grade school & even high school first. There you could learn French, Astronomy, and about other countries around the world.

Most likely I'll be home by the time you can read this letter, and then I'll be able to tell you a whole bunch of stories about my travels. That is if you don't eat this letter while you're teething, or tear it up or do some terrible thing to it that would make it illegible (hard to read).

After the job is over, maybe two or three months, I'm moving to Southern California to live with my old friend (David is his name). We'll build the boat there. It would be kind of dumb to build a boat in Colorado, in the mountains I mean. You'd have to build it on roller skates & ride in it down some highway until ... SPLASH !!! You hit water.

Anyway, I guess I'm the first one ever to write you a letter. Your mom probably opened it already, but I wanted her to do it. It's kind of a letter for her too.

Brothers & sisters fight a lot when they're young. Then they get older & they go their separate ways. When all of a sudden you miss them maybe because you'll never be able to fight with anyone else like you did with them. Then you see them all too little & they have babies & stuff like that & you might not see them too often 'cause you're too far away. Nevertheless you love them all.

A lot of Love,

Uncle Danny

Dan had made up his mind to head to Southern California. He had never been there, it was close to the sea, and he knew he'd be welcomed. David had his family's blessing prior to inviting Dan to California—only a formality so that Dan wouldn't show up on the Bull's doorstep entirely unexpected. But even if he had, David said, it would have been OK with everyone.

So, with David's invitation and full approval from the rest of the Bull family, Dan finished his job in Denver, said goodbye to his friends and roommates at the University Avenue house, and set off on his next adventure.

Having already spent considerable time exploring the Front Range west of Denver, Dan steered his motorbike southwestward, and avoided interstates as best he could. He followed back roads out of Colorado, worked his way through Monument Valley down to Flagstaff, Arizona, camping along the way. It was slow going. A hot, bone-breaking ride on an underpowered street bike with a Gibson acoustic guitar strapped to the pillion seat. By the time he got to California, historic Route 66 would be his best option across the Mojave Desert. He would have ridden past the desolate spot where he would lose his life only three months later.

In mid-July, Dan arrived in Tustin to be welcomed by members of his second family he hadn't seen since his last visit to The Homestead five summers earlier.

The Bull's Tustin property was less than a half-acre, had a kidney-shaped pool, a pond with goldfish, a volleyball court, and a buried underground bomb shelter in the backyard, which Uncle Bob, true to form, had tasked David with excavating.

David had spent his freshman and sophomore years at Northern Arizona University in Flagstaff. David's closer friends at school had either graduated or moved on to other schools by the end of his second year in 1973. For assorted reasons, including reducing the cost of college by no longer paying out-of-state tuition, David had transferred to University of California at Irvine for one quarter. UC-Irvine was geared more toward science than the English and literature degree Dave had been pursuing, so, on the advice of a friend of Martha's, he transferred to Cal State-Fullerton. Dave would commute to school from home his last couple of years of college. His quarters at the Tustin home, shared with Dan that summer, was a one-room shack with bunkbeds across the pool from the house. It had electricity but no indoor plumbing.

By the time Dan arrived in California, the experimental drug phase of his college years was very much behind him, and David had never delved deeply into the sport. There were other priorities. They both had jobs that summer in boatyards. David had begun training in Tae Kwon Do in Flagstaff and attended sessions three or four nights a week after getting off work at the small sailboat factory he worked at in Irvine. Dave invited Dan to join him at the dojo. However, having landed a job in a boat building factory in Costa Mesa as a carpenter and working part time at a grocery store, Dan was too busy. Moreover, he'd connected with a coworker who was also into motorbikes, and the two headed into the desert to ride their machines together. David and Dan still spent time together and found time to party, but it was mostly alcohol with a little pot mixed in, recreational, and not often. They had other priorities. There was work. There were dreams!

"It seems everything Danny spoke about," recalls David, "well, it turns out he was right. The way he was living his life turned out to be right. 'You should get out and enjoy this world,' Dan would say. I used to get on him about his cigarettes. I'd say, 'Danny, I wish you weren't a smoker. Those things are going to kill you.'"

Danny would look right back at David and say, "Dave, it's not going to matter." After getting the same response more than once, David dropped the subject.

August 28, 1974

Dear Danny,

Late or not, I was most appreciative of your card on my birthday. I thank you very much.

I hope this note gets to you—I am aware that David is now back in California, so maybe your plans are more firm now. At any rate, I'm sure you enjoyed the West coast and had a great job experience while you were there. If you choose to come to Chicago—you know you are most welcome, anytime, for as long as you would like to stay.

Your boat idea seems like a pretty ambitious one. Mom ran into Bill and Barb Armstrong the other day. They have sold their home in Forest Lake and have purchased a farmhouse and barn way out in the country—they did this so Bill could realize a lifelong ambition. They are using the barn to build a 40-foot sailboat in, which Bill has wanted to do for quite some time. Perhaps if your boat idea does not happen now—it will in the future just as Bill is doing now.

As you know, Den and Deb have bought a home, it's up on the hill in Baraboo. It's a real nice place and very comfortable. Our family gave them a lawnmower for a housewarming, not very creative or exciting, but it was something they needed and wanted.

Sarah Lynn is an absolute doll. She amazes everyone because she is so active, she smiles all the time and just seems to love everyone. Debbie is so beautiful and so aware of life, she keeps us well informed of Sarah's accomplishments, we know to the minute when she first sat up by herself, when she cut her first teeth, etc., etc. She makes having a granddaughter very exciting.

Mr. Terry of course is in the middle of his Senate race, an activity that everyone in the family seems to somewhat disapprove of at this time. Well, I'm sure things will happen for the best for all concerned.

Your brother is fine. He has found many new fine friends and has a great enjoyment for all he does. He is as tall as I am and must weigh 155. You would be quite proud of him.

We are all very proud of you, my friend. Everyone speaks so highly of you, always and without exception. Of course we miss you very much, think of you often, and hope and pray that you are happy, content, and in good health.

Mom and I are still creaking around. She is having another problem and will probably have another operation late this month. Everything considered, this is probably best, she has been so very uncomfortable lately, more than she can really stand.

Please let us hear from you, write when you can and call anytime. If we can ever help or console, realize we will try our best to assist and understand—anytime. We love and miss you and of course wish you were closer to us, both in miles and in all other ways possible.

My love,

Dad

According to Aunt Connie, Dan was the perfect houseguest. He brought her flowers and was thoughtful in ways that her own family was not. He helped Aunt Connie with many odd jobs around the house, did his own laundry, and other various chores. He even started cooking once a week, preparing dishes he'd picked up in Denver and during his travels.

September 20th, 1974

Dear Mom,

Me and California don't get along very well. At least southern California is not where I really want to live for the next 5 years, much less a couple more months. So I'm leaving.

Dave and I got along well through the past few months. We'll get together maybe after school is out.

Anyway, you might be happy to find out I'm not traveling by motorcycle this time. "My God I bought a car," is what I said. I feel a terrible sense of fear about owning another.

Anyway I bought the '57 Volkswagen Bus. I had to buy one to move all my stuff around in.

I guess I'll go to Mexico this week or next weekend. After that I'm heading to northern California maybe to look for another job in a boatyard. I'll have about $800 or so after I buy the van, pay insurance, etc.

If I work, I could also take a course in boat design. I have the work permits for work in New Zealand where they pioneered the type of boat I'd like to build. I may get granted a job in N.Z. if it works out. I'd be there for a year. Gotta write to the "ferrocement" limited in Aukland first. Anyway if things don't work in northern California, I'm headed for Colorado for a couple of months then home in November, maybe?

Anyway I'm leaving S. California. I hope you're happy 'cause I am. Too many people around, no fresh air.

I hear that you're gonna have an "all American," as Uncle Bob puts it. He is still the same old Bob Bull. I suppose you know that. See if they'll give you a lifetime guarantee on this one. You should not buy anything that expensive without a warranty of some kind.

Seriously, I hope it is the last time you gotta go in the hospital for many moons.

I guess Debbie and Denis' Wedding Anniversary is coming up soon. Maybe I'll be back by then. For sure by Christmas. I guess they're really digging it in the house, I'd like to see what they do to it, Deb has such a talent to make a house look good. I owe her a letter too.

Love much, Take care,

Danny

P.S. I'll try and write from Mexico

Dan would soon be moving on again. That much was apparent. His dreams of further travel were still up in the air, but he was clearly done with Southern California, as indicated by this letter home, written ten days before his death.

David was already back at school at Cal State-Fullerton in September 1974, about to get his degree. Danny may have felt some personal regret seeing his childhood friend and quasi-brother, a school year younger, on the verge of earning his college degree.

Bob Schneider graduated earlier that year. I could see Dan saying to himself, "I have traveled, I will travel again—but first, let's go to Denver, mull things over, and then go back home and get this school thing done."

Dan's experiment with California was over. He had traveled from coast to coast on more than one continent, maybe more than two. His curiosity with California may have been over not long after he had arrived. He had tried Southern California to see if it might fit, but it wasn't for him. The Los Angeles smog of the seventies was new to him, and he hated it. It wasn't the California celebrated in song by the Beach Boys in the sixties. Moreover, everyone in the Bull world was moving on with their lives. David headed back to school, still attending martial arts classes. Martha was working with plans unclear. Leslie was off to Pepperdine for her freshman year. Like me, Julie was a sophomore in high school. Uncle Bob buried himself in his job at Fender Guitar, and Aunt Connie worked hard to support everyone's busy schedule. Although a welcome guest, it was time for Dan to go.

At home, the intensity of the father-son firestorm had subsided, or so it seemed. Our father had finally accepted that Dan would sort things out and "find himself" in his own time, his own way. Dan had been away from Illinois for the better part of two years now and had proved that whatever came his way, he was up for the challenge. He wasn't coming back to ride his father's coattails. He would continue to chase his dreams and forge his own path.

Dan looked to return to Illinois. His letters at the time suggested as much. David and Martha said the same in our interviews. About two weeks before he left California, Dan spoke by phone with Bob Schneider. Bob confirmed Dan was on a trajectory toward home. He had asked Dan, "Why are you coming back home?"

Dan's response: "Because I have this dream [his dream of building a sailboat and sailing the world], and it's a good dream, but it's not a real dream. I'm coming home because I miss my family."

Bob added, "He missed the collective us. His family and friends in Illinois. He had been gone for a long time."

Dan likely would have stopped in Denver and, perhaps in Utah along the way to see Richard Menzies, but he was on his way home. What would have happened once he got there, as far as his future, was anyone's guess.

My father shared something with me when I was a young boy. It left an impression, even at that age, that a father could have such a conversation with his nine-year-old son. One evening, sitting near the picture window overlooking Diamond Lake, he said, "Son, if I make mistakes in raising you, please forgive me. My father was gone when I was very young, so I don't have a mentor or a template to measure myself by."

This was years before Danny's death and before any big conflict had arisen between them. It may have been prophetic. Navigating the late-sixties and early-seventies (the Vietnam years), my father strived, as most fathers do, to improve his children's lives and prospects. Danny was trying to assure him that he had done so: provided ample opportunity in life to pursue dreams, his dreams.

Martha had arrived back in Tustin in early August, having spent most of the summer living in Salt Lake City, waitressing downtown during the week and on weekends working on the Heber Valley Railroad tourist train. Dan and Martha hadn't seen one another since 1969, when

Dan was sixteen and Martha was fourteen. They had known each other well growing up, and when Martha arrived in Tustin, she and Dan had an immediate intense connection. They kept it very proper, but their relationship became more intimate as they sought each other out in their free time.

The two had many deep conversations that Martha found relatable. Dan felt that he had disappointed his father by not following the standard road to success. Martha, at the time, was unsure of her direction in life and sensed similar disapproval from her overachieving father. In Martha, Dan found a more sympathetic ear than he would've found with Dave. Dave knew there were conflicts between Danny and his dad, but Dan didn't discuss those issues with Dave, for good reason. In David's words: "There wasn't gonna be much tarnishing of Uncle Dan in my eyes, and Danny knew it." David adored our father—he was quite different from his own.

Dan and David had already planned a trip to Mexico to whoop it up before Dan packed and hit the road. Coastal Mexico would be another exotic destination for Dan to add to his travel resume.

"David is a cool brother and friend," Martha told us. "He included me in things all the time growing up."

September 29 was also Martha's birthday. The boys invited her to join them on their weekend getaway to Mexico in Dan's used 1957 VW bus. David, a good student, spoke Spanish fluently. The three made a couple of stops in Tijuana before heading to Hussong's Cantina in Ensenada to drink tequila and have themselves some fun.

The "Mexican Feds" (Federales) had hassled David on previous trips to Mexico, confiscating eight-track tapes and other personal property as bribes to leave Dave alone, so the three were careful to avoid the authorities as they looked for a place to camp south of Ensenada that night.

As they worked their way toward the coast on a dirt road, they came across a local kid, and David used his language skills to get the lay of the land. It turned out they were on the kid's family farm. David asked for directions to the beach and whether there might be any Federales patrolling the area. The kid told them he hadn't seen any "Feds" around and pointed them toward the beach. The three camped for the weekend on the beach with the waves of the Pacific crashing before them.

"It was unbelievably cool," Martha said. "No one in sight up and down the beach. We didn't see another soul the entire time we were there."

Saturday morning, Dave and Dan explored the beach while Martha stayed behind. No one was around, so she decided, with some urging from Dan before they left, to enjoy the morning sun and work on her all-over tan until they returned.

"One of the best feelings of my life," Martha recalled. "I felt so uninhibited and freed from social norms."

She had the time of her life with her two favorite men at the time. Thrilled to be included on an adventure with a brother she'd always admired and a life-long friend with whom she was falling in love.

"You can't imagine how much of a good time I was having. Dan and I were playfully intimate the whole weekend without flaunting it in front of David," Martha said. "I don't think he knew anything was going on between Dan and me. If he did know, and I don't know how he couldn't have had a few suspicions, it has never been talked about. It was a wonderful weekend in a beautiful setting, I wish I'd brought my camera.

"The world tilted after that weekend—David and I haven't talked about it since. You know how David is. He has never really talked about that time at all except for when he had to talk to the police."

The trio got back to Tustin late Sunday evening, Martha's birthday. Monday, Dan went shopping and Martha joined him on his errands.

"We went to Radio Shack, the drug store, you know, getting stuff! Preparing for the road," Martha said.

While shopping that day, Dan invited Martha to join him on the road, but Martha wasn't prepared to run off with him. He didn't know exactly what his plan was, and that wasn't very alluring. The fire of romance and the allure of the road was strong, and she gave it some thought before deciding it wasn't for her.

Later that day, Dave and Dan hit a little place for a glass of wine and to say their goodbyes. By early evening, Dan was packed and ready to push off with his other family, minus Leslie, gathered at his van. David said, "See ya, bro." Julie gave a big hug. Aunt Connie, who always loved Dan like a son, bade him farewell. Martha offered a wink and a goodbye kiss.

Uncle Bob pleaded with Danny to stay one more night and leave in the morning, but Dan declined.

Uncle Bob said, "If you get back to Illinois and friction remains between you and your dad, our door here in California is always open." He added, "If you get tired, please, pull over and rest."

Uncle Bob stood beside the van when Danny left.

"I think as he was pulling out of the driveway, I was following and yelling, 'Please change your mind!' I was very much opposed to what he was doing (leaving at that late hour). We felt like he was a member of the family at that point and didn't want to lose him. I didn't want him to leave thinking he had worn out his welcome. We were sincere in our begging him to stay. He had become an even more important part of our lives."

Though Dan's mental compass was pointing toward Denver, his route and itinerary weren't decided. At least he wouldn't have to sleep on the cold, hard ground like he had three months earlier on the way to California. He now had the relative comfort and safety of his van.

Ear and Eyewitness

We had been sitting in the back of THE SHACK, Ken listening to the events that had led Dan to Cajon pass that night. Since our first contact, Ken had avoided sharing any "details" of that October 1 morning. All I knew was what the police had told us and what I had read in articles. I was now prepared to hear what transpired in the Mojave Desert that morning from the person who was there.

"Tell me what happened to you that morning, Ken. I'm ready." I braced myself.

Ken seemed as if he were waiting for permission to open up.

"First," he said, "I need to ask you a question. Do you have any suspicion that I had anything to do with Dan being murdered? Another reason I haven't talked about it over the years is, early on, when I did open up, I was asked by a couple of people if I had anything to do with it. That messes me up. I could never do somethin' like that, and for someone to think I could, well, it really hurts."

I looked at him and replied, "Even before last month when we were put in touch, I had trusted that the authorities, my father, and Uncle Bob had done their due diligence, so I have never thought seriously that you had anything to do with Dan's murder. Where did you bury the shotguns and where is the shovel? Why did you stay behind to help Dan? That was before I knew the Tommy Sanford story and how you came to be in

California and at Cajon Pass in the first place."

Ken nodded and said, "Thank you."

When Ken jumped into the back of Dan's van early that morning, he felt all was right with the world.

"I put my bag of clothes and bowling ball bag next to me and laid on my back comfortably on Dan's bedroll. I was with someone I believed was safe and I was either on my way to Denver with this guy I just met, or I would at least be closer to Texas by the time we parted ways, and the hitchhiking would be easier. I fell asleep in no time at all.

"I was jolted awake by the gunshot, or let's say a loud noise. It must have been the first shot that woke me, but I don't know for sure. It had to be the first shot or first two shots simultaneously going off."

Ken said it sounded like a Gatling gun going off, with the pellets ricocheting all over the inside of Dan's VW.

"Those blasts messed up my left ear. To this day, I still have some trouble hearing out of this ear." Ken tugged his left earlobe. "Also, loud bangs send me instantly into an anxiety attack.

"Then, and it still gets to me, I heard Dan plea for his life. 'Man, don't shoot me.'"

Those were Dan's last words, published by law enforcement and the media years ago. What Ken had heard and remembered in *that* moment. The only last words we had known until I met Ken thirty-six years later. I now preferred to remember Dan's last words being, "I'm just going to sit up here and catch the sunrise."

"Then came another blast, and another right behind it," Ken said. "Chunks of glass flew everywhere. I could smell the gunpowder. I was lyin' on my back, my head at the bottom center rear of the VW bench seat. My feet were toward the back of the van and Dan's motorcycle. I saw his head jerk back when the second shots hit. His long hair flew from the wind force of the shotgun blasts. I saw blood hit the ceiling of the van."

Ken stopped to gather himself. Understandably. I'm sure he hadn't shared this much detail in a long time, if ever. I felt bad, but I still wanted to know. Dan's murder was gruesome. He was shot four times with 12-gauge shotguns at close range, through glass. I had already assumed the scene was ugly. Ugly enough for Uncle Bob to recommend a closed casket to my father.

Ken said, "I didn't know what was going on. My mind was racing. What was happening? Was my driver wanted by the law and the police just shot him? Nothing about that made sense. My mind was clipping off possibilities when the realization hit me. My life was in danger, too."

Ken took a sip of water and a deep breath.

"A cold sweat broke out all over my body. I propped myself up on my elbow and peeked around the wall on the driver's side. The blonde guy with the bandana was standing right there, just a couple of feet away, lookin' straight at me, it seemed. I anticipated the back door of the van to fly open. I had a blanket over me, and I remember grabbin' my bowling ball bag and holdin' it in front of me to stop the gunshots coming my way. The handle to the sliding back door jiggled, but the door didn't open and them shots never came. I just laid there, not sure if I was even breathing."

Ken said he heard footsteps move away from the van. He was drowning in sweat, like someone had poured a bucket of water over him. It was dripping in his eyes. He slowly put his bowling ball bag down and moved as quietly as he could until he was able to peek above the bench seat next to the wall on the driver's side. He saw two men. One was about twenty feet away, walking toward the highway at his twelve o'clock. The other, bandana guy, stopped about ten feet away at his eleven. Ken used his hands to make sure we had the orientation he was describing.

"The guy at my eleven, blonde bandana guy, looked back at the van, right at me again. It was close to sunrise—maybe there was a reflection off our windshield that hindered his view, I don't know. He looked right at me, holdin' a shotgun by his side in his right hand. I was sure he saw me this time, but then he turned and started walkin' toward the highway with the other guy."

Ken took sip of water.

"The way they walked away from Dan's van has always struck me. They were so casual. It were as if they were goin' to get an ice cream or somethin'. They were so nonchalant. I only ever saw the one shotgun in the blonde guy's hand. It was a single barrel. Couldn't tell if it was auto or pump. I ducked back down to the floor of Dan's van. I heard their van start up. It was about seventy-five yards away on the shoulder of Interstate 40, also at about my eleven o' clock. I heard them drive away.

"I was confused, scared, shaking, and drenched. My mind was going, 'What the hell just happened?' My heart was beating out of my chest. It seemed like an eternity had passed before I reached and tried to open the side door of the VW. Even though I had heard them drive off, I was still terrified. As quietly as possible, I jiggled the handle. I hadn't used that door yet. I couldn't get the door to slide open. It was probably locked, and I didn't know how to unlock it. I panicked. I knew Dan needed help.

"I started to climb over the bench seat and over Dan. He was shot up bad. I reached passed Dan with my fingertips and opened the driver's side door. I slid over the seat, over Dan, and onto the ground outside the van. He had been sitting upright in the center of the bench seat with his legs toward the floor of the passenger's seat. I knocked him over as I tried to get out of the van. I made sure his head was out of the way when I shut the VW door behind me. It was about twenty to forty yards to the highway. I ran to the shoulder and tried to wave down help."

"The fellow who helped you?" Loretta asked. "Was it one or two guys who helped you get Dan's body to Needles?"

Ken sort of disregarded the question and continued his description of that morning.

"The first car to stop was this Marine. My gosh, nobody would stop for the longest time, or at least it sure seemed like a long time. I was standin' on the side of the road and jumpin' out into the road tryin' to get somebody to stop. There were trucks going by at seventy to eighty miles per hour blowing their horns at me, some just missing me, and no one would stop. I had no idea what I looked like, but people must have thought a crazy man had escaped from the asylum and he was hanging out in the middle of the Mojave Desert at 6 a.m. on a Tuesday."

Ken paused briefly to reflect, shaking his head.

"I most likely wouldn't have stopped for me, even in my most crazy days. God bless the guy who did because once he stopped, others were willing to stop and help, too. It was that Marine, his wife, and his two kids who were in the first car stop."

"He stopped with his wife and two kids?" Loretta said. "Wow, that surprises me. But he was a Marine. My brother served as a Marine, so maybe I shouldn't be surprised. He could probably handle himself. Still, with a family, that took guts, no matter who you are."

Ken nodded.

"When they stopped, I went to their car. I hadn't given any thought to what I looked like. I went to the car and leaned in toward the window of the passenger side, talkin' across his wife. I said, 'Sir, you might want to get out of the car to hear what I got to say.' I saw fear in the eyes of his wife in the passenger seat. She looked petrified, and the Marine looked scared, too. Understandably so, for sure. I was freakin' out, I was shaking. I'm shaking just telling you about this."

Ken went silent to gain his composure, and continued, "I said to the Marine, 'I'm not gonna hurt you or rob you or anything. That's not what's goin' on here. A guy gave me a ride last night, and he's been shot. I need help.'

"The Marine got out of his car and walked around to the passenger's side. He was still very guarded and positioned himself between me and his family in the car. 'Do you know first aid?' He asks. I go, 'Yeah, I do!'

I took off runnin' back toward the shot-up VW, but I stopped dead in my tracks after just a few steps."

Ken paused again.

"I really didn't know anything about first aid back then. I had picked up pieces here and there from my dad growin' up, but what I knew about first aid was not gonna help Dan in any way. I don't know why I said that to the Marine. Lack of sleep, the red-hot heat of the moment. I was in a daze, not thinking clearly. I turned and walked back to the Marine. 'I don't know first aid. Do you?' He said he did and then left his family and followed me to the VW van. 'He's dead,' I told the Marine as we approached the van. 'I know he's dead.'"

"The wife and kids stayed in the car?" Loretta asked.

"Yeah, they never got out of the car," Ken confirmed. "By the time the Marine and I checked on Dan and got back to the highway, these people from Weatherford, Texas, had stopped. They must've seen me with the Marine on the side of the road and sensed that there was a situation, and they could help. I just remember them suddenly being there with their helping hands. It was an older man and his wife. They had a pickup truck with a topper-camper on the back. The three of us men went and got Dan and put him in the back of that truck, in the camper. I got in back too. Dan and I rode together in the back of that camper to the Needles hospital."

"Danny was dead?" I asked.

Ken nodded, looking me straight in the eyes.

"Dan was dead when we lifted him out of the van. I'm sure of it. He was shot up real bad. It pains me to say it this way, but Dan was mostly likely beyond saving moments after the shots."

Ken cleared his throat.

"That must have been the longest hour of your life," I said. "As you know, we took that ride from where you and Dan parked that night to Needles, about a month ago. This was before we knew you and this much more of the story. My heart goes out to you, and I thank you, for staying with my brother."

Ken nodded again.

He probably didn't have much choice but to ride in back with Dan. It didn't matter. Ken couldn't unsee it. He couldn't unfeel what he felt during that hour.

"What about the report that some truck driver with a CB reported things?" I asked.

"I think you're right about that. A trucker had pulled up. But I also think the folks we were ridin' with had a CB. I'm not sure but I'm pretty sure. By the time we got outside of Needles, there was a highway patrolman behind us, lights spinnin', the whole thing, but he was just keeping pace with us. I was lookin' out the camper window when he pulled in behind us, and I wondered why we weren't pullin' over to tell this policeman what was goin' on. I found out when we got to the hospital that they had been communicating over CB."

From a private investigator's report, not a police report: "A trucker who had a radio transmitter in his vehicle reported the incident. Both the victim and the hitchhiker were gone from the scene when police arrived."

Ken said, "We pulled into the hospital in Needles, and I found out there had been a cop leading and escorting our camper in addition to the cop following. The medical staff was at the back of the truck immediately, attending to me asking, 'Where are you shot?' I'm screaming, 'I'm not the one who is shot! Help him, help Dan!'

"They turned to Dan and began to unload his body from the back of the camper and onto a gurney. The next thing someone says, it may have been a cop, I don't know, everything was so confusing and happening so fast. I had just rode an hour with Dan's dead body by my side and I hear, 'Why'd you shoot him?' I looked around. No one else answered, and everyone was lookin' in my direction."

"I said, 'I didn't shoot him! What's is wrong with you people? I didn't shoot anyone! That man gave me a ride last night. I'm trying to save him!'"

Ken was becoming increasingly emotional and animated.

"That was around the time I realized what I looked like. Things calmed down. I needed to use the bathroom. I was escorted into the hospital by a nurse and a cop. One of the nurses scrounged up a change of clothes, where from, I have no idea. They almost fit. Once in the bathroom, I looked in the mirror and saw this scared, skinny kid with eyes as wide as silver dollars. I was covered in blood."

Ken looked down at the table, shaking his head.

"When I climbed over Dan, his blood soaked my clothes. I looked fresh out of a horror movie. Blood on my face, hands, everywhere. It was no wonder no one would stop on the highway. It was no wonder folks in the hospital parking lot were looking at me the way they did."

You read about awful events like this, I thought. We've all seen appalling stories in fictionalized and non-fictionalized forms often. But what Ken was describing, this nonfiction story, happened to us. I don't know why I asked the next question. Maybe to close the loop or just to add some levity to our tense conversation.

"Did you still have the Skoal can on you?" I asked.

Ken grinned. "Yeah. I had already stashed my rollin' papers under a cushion in those kind people's camper that took Dan and me to Needles. I still had the Skoal can in my jeans when I was in the bathroom viewing the horror in the mirror. For some bone-headed reason, I kept it on me even after I changed my clothes. I was at the hospital for two or three hours before they took me to the highway patrol station. I remember hearing and seeing helicopters circling in the distance. I heard them off and on for the rest of the time I was in the area.

"The highway patrol station must have been right around the corner. I barely remember going there except for hearing the helicopters. That's what sticks in my mind. I was at the hospital and then—BAM!—I was at the patrol station. The first thing I asked to do when we got to the highway patrol station was to use the bathroom. I flushed the contents of the Skoal can down the toilet and tossed the can in the garbage.

"I was in Needles till about sunset. Still at the highway patrol station or sheriff's station, I don't know. I just remember this facility out in the middle of the desert somewhere."

Ken looked at me and said, "You were just in Needles. It's just a little town in the desert—there's not much there as I recall. Did you see the facility I'm describing?"

I responded, "That's pretty much Needles today, but all we did was follow the hospital signs and pull into the parking lot to form a better picture in our heads. We didn't even think of looking for the highway patrol station."

"I'd have to go back there to recognize the buildings," said Ken. "But thirty-six years later, it has likely changed a lot."

"I don't know, Ken," I said. "Needles is likely to be similar to the way it was back then. It is a smaller town along Interstate 40, probably not that much different than places where you grew up. If your memory of Needles is based upon that one day when you were there in 1974, I don't know how you would remember anything about the town."

Ken nodded. "Yeah, you're probably right," he said. "Anyway, that police station or highway patrol station is where they took me after the hospital. That's where they held me most of the day. Later in the evening, two cops took me back to where Dan was shot. We met up with two detectives from San Bernardino. I suspect they had been out at the scene most of the day goin' over Dan's van lookin' for evidence. The two detectives took me to San Bernardino and they put me up in a hotel. I think it was called The Sundowner. I don't know why I'd remember somethin' that trivial, but I'm pretty sure it was The Sundowner. Weird, huh?"

Ken shook his head.

"Also, my bowling ball bag and bag of clothes showed up sometime that night. When and how, again, I have no idea or just can't remember."

"So that pretty much confirms the fact that the police didn't believe you had anything to do with Dan's murder, putting you up at a hotel?" I asked.

"I obviously wasn't a suspect in their minds, at least not a serious suspect. Otherwise, they would have thought I was a flight risk and put me up that night in their jail."

Ken paused. "Gosh, that night, the nightmare for me just continued. I still hadn't slept but for just a few hours in the last seventy-two, and I hadn't slept in what could be called a real bed in weeks. That night, whether it was real or not, it was real to me, all that night, I would see guys walkin' past the window and in the shadows with shotguns, *all night*! Whether they were real or not, I saw them! I got outta bed and sat in a corner of my hotel room with the lights off. I just sat there and kept watch 'til almost dawn. Finally, exhausted, I did get into the bed, but I was still keepin' that one eye open, monitoring the door and window. If I slept that night, it was only in fits and starts, as they say."

Ken took a long pause and a drink of water.

"Couldn't tell you the time, and I couldn't tell you if it was prearranged. I think the detectives just showed up the next mornin'. We started driving to the San Bernardino courthouse. The detectives asked me questions, more or less quizzing me. Inserting untruths, changing the story. I believe they were testing me on facts they had already deciphered from Dan's van and the crime scene. They had taken their gloves off. They should! They do that to try to get to the truth. I just wish it hadn't been me on the receiving end of the interrogation."

Loretta and I nodded.

"So they take me into the courthouse," Ken continued. "They tell me we're goin' upstairs to give you a lie detector test. I go, 'What! Why? I don't know what to tell 'em.'"

They asked, "What do you mean?"

Ken was showing stress again, his voice getting lower, harder to hear.

"Like I told them yesterday, the back door of the van was locked. I had to climb over the driver's seat and Dan's body to get out of the van. When I opened the door, Dan's upper body fell out of the van. I had to lift his torso and put him back in the van to shut the door. You're gonna ask me, I know you're goin' to ask me if I killed him, and that's all I'm gonna to see, Dan's limp torso hangin' out of that van. That needle on that machine, the lie detector, it's gonna go haywire. I'm not goin' to be in control when you ask me if I killed him.

"Then they messed with me again. They told me they weren't gonna ask me that question."

Ken paused, drew a deep breath.

"'What we are going to do,' the detectives said, 'is ask you a series of questions, and we're going to ask you these questions over and over again, but we're going to put them in different order.'

"That's pretty much what happened. They did this series of questions like maybe three, maybe four times, and the last time through, out of the blue, they asked, 'Did you kill Dan Walker?' I said no, and the lie detector test was over."

Ken leaned back in his chair.

"So I'm done with the lie detector, and I'm sittin' in this room waitin' for the results of the test. This beautiful bombshell blond lady in a police uniform comes over and throws a magazine on the table. 'Maybe this will take your mind off of things,' she says.

"I'm sure I looked like an ice cube on a fryin' pan. I never had a lie detector test before. I really hadn't slept in a long time, not to mention everything else going on. I never touched that magazine.

"After a while, the gray-haired detective comes in with his partner behind him, and I go, 'So what's the deal?' And he looks at me and goes, 'Looks like we have a pretty honest young man here. We're going to let you go.'

"I stood, pumped my fist, and let out a good Texas 'Yeehaw!'

"But then, I sat back down and said, 'I'll tell you what. I'm not leaving here until y'all get me a ride home. I'm not leaving here. I'm not hitchhiking, I don't have the money to get home, and my mom's in the hospital. *I'm not leaving here until you get me a ride home!*'

"After what I had been through, there was no way I was sticking my thumb out again. I was dead serious, and they could tell.

"The detectives reimbursed me for some food I'd bought in Needles and while hanging around waitin' for the lie detector test in San Bernardino. I pretty much still had the $60 I won playin' pool seemingly ages ago at the NCO's club with Tommy.

"That afternoon, the detectives took me to a truck stop near Barstow. We went into the restaurant, got a table, and they let me order some food on their tab. They started canvassing the truck stop restaurant. I wasn't sure what was up. It wasn't too long before they returned to the table with these two guys, truck drivers—a young weathered Spanish Floridian and an older Cajun guy in his forties. Those southern truckers came back to the table with the detectives and, being polite folks from the South, asked me to take off my Tennessee Gambler's hat. My hair was long back then, and all messed up, so it was not an improvement. The detectives introduced me to the men and said, 'These two truck drivers are going to take you back to Abilene.'

"Those guys treated me like a kid they needed to take care of. Kept me under their wings, you could say. They were really good guys. I'm sure the detectives tried to vet my next ride the best they could. They'd told the truckers the situation, what I'd been through. Other than a couple of stops off the beaten path onto some farms to pick up shipments of oranges, which I helped load, and a couple of meal and fuel breaks, those two truckers had me at the truck stop in Abilene safe and sound within about 48 hours. I can't put into words how relieved I was to get back to Abilene, home."

"Wow," I said.

Loretta said, "And the world was a different place for you."

"Very different," answered Ken. "I called my brother, Don, from a payphone to come pick me up. We came here to THE SHACK and got drunk, breaking my promise to God."

The World Tilts

*"There are certain things
you try not to think about
when you close your eyes at night.
Danny is one of those things
I purposely try not to think or talk about.
I would never sleep otherwise."
R.P. Bull (Uncle Bob)*

Martha believed she was the first in her home to get the call from authorities the day after Dan left. She was the only one at home when she went into her parent's room to answer the phone call that Tuesday.

"I couldn't believe it. I was in disbelief!" she said. "You must be mistaken!" She questioned the police.

They described the van, said the occupant's name was Dan Walker, and that there was a motorcycle in back along with a hitchhiker he had picked up earlier that evening.

"I confirmed to the police that Dan had just left our house the night before and he had been living with us," Martha said. "After that, shock just set in. I remember darkness, and I have no other memories of who I communicated with or what else happened that night. I blanked out."

My best guess was she gave the authorities her father's work number, and they called Uncle Bob at Fender.

When we asked David where he was when he got the news, he said he used to visit his dad's office to use the phone and study after his classes at Cal State-Fullerton a few times a month. Uncle Bob's office and the factories for Fender Guitars, Rhodes Piano, and Rogers Drums were also in Fullerton. David was sitting in his father's office when the phone rang. A look of dread came immediately over his father's face as authorities delivered the news. Uncle Bob hung up and called Illinois to deliver the bad news, news he didn't want his old friend hearing from anyone but him. Thirty-six years later, I learned we were both with our fathers as this exchange took place.

Uncle Bob and Dave barely spoke before Uncle Bob left for San Bernardino to confirm the victim was, indeed, Dan. He drove to the morgue in San Bernardino by himself. That's when he must have brushed by Ken at some point.

When we interviewed Uncle Bob, I asked the foolish question, "Were you in shock?"

The wiser eighty-two-year-old answered. "I don't know, Douglas. When you are in a state of shock, do you know it?"

Then he added, "There are certain things I try not to think about when I close my eyes at night. Danny is one of those things I purposely try not to think or talk about. I would never sleep otherwise. When I do think about it, everything is so vivid, from saying goodbye to Dan in the driveway and begging him to stay at least one more night to having to drive to the San Bernardino sheriff's office to confirm it was him. If these thoughts are on my mind as I try to sleep, I don't sleep—therefore, I don't care to remember."

Law enforcement converged upon the Bulls' home on Lemona Lane, peppering everyone in the family with questions. Leslie was at school, so she was spared the inquisition.

The police grilled David and forced him to give up anyone he knew who was involved, even to the smallest degree, in the drug trade. He told us, "They were suspecting me, my friends, questioning my sister Martha, and investigating possible business grievances against my father."

"The FBI showed up and everything," Martha recalled. They probed her relationship with Dan, as well as other personal details.

"Were you and Danny lovers?" the FBI asked.

They were suggesting platonic friends and schoolmates of Martha's of being jealous boyfriends and involved in Dan's murder.

"Are you pregnant?" they asked.

"No!" she had said, explaining that she and Dan had never taken their relationship that far.

"I felt ganged up on. There were two or three of them saying crazy things and making all these horrible insinuations."

Uncle Bob and Aunt Connie flew to Illinois as soon they could book a flight. Despite dealing with their own grief, they were the rocks in my parents' life that week. They instructed their kids to stay home in California so they could focus on supporting and comforting their longtime friends.

The only "nourishment" I recalled my parents consuming that week was Scotch and water in the evenings and orange soda during the day. I also had my first drink of alcohol that week. My most crazy and controversial cousin poured me a shot of tequila and ordered me to down it. I did as I was told.

Days later, the police released Dan's possessions from the van and delivered them to the Bull residence on Lemona Lane, all of which ended up laid out in the garage on the ping pong table like used items in a yard sale.

"That ass had stolen my Siddhartha book," Martha recalled. "That book had my name written in it. Dan had also taken one of my belts that had my name on it. In those first moments, I was mad but then I laughed.

I was then touched when I realized Dan had lifted small mementos from each of us to hold onto until we would see each other again."

Like many of those closest to Dan, Martha went into a dark place. Hers lasted for about a year.

"A horrible place. I cried and cried and cried. I was completely devastated. All my friends knew. I wasn't taking care of myself. I didn't care about anything. The deepest depression I've ever experienced in my life and, to a degree, suicidal. Did I let Dan down by saying no to his invitation to join him on the road? If I had gone, would things have turned out differently?"

Sometime later, after the police released Dan's van, we offered it to David. My father had washed his hands of it and asked Uncle Bob to take care of getting rid of it once the police released it. Dave declined the offer.

"I was already having bad dreams. I didn't ever want to see the outside of the vehicle, much less the inside. That could only make my dreams that much worse."

Westsail Corporation / 1638 Placentia Avenue / Costa Mesa, California 92627 / (714) XXX-XXXX/
October 4, 1974
R.P. Bull
Tustin, CA

Dear Mr. Bull,

The news of Dan's passing reached us here at Westsail this morning and created an immediate feeling of shocked disbelief.

I hired Dan and was his immediate supervisor for the majority of the time he was employed here. During this time I found Dan to be a fine man and a gifted, if relatively inexperienced, craftsman. He talked often of building his own boat and sailing off to pursue the dream of most of us who love boats and the sea.

During the time that Dan, "Colorado," was here at Westsail, he made many friends, and his leaving to return to Colorado left a void in our gang that will be hard to fill.

Even though "Colorado" will not be here with us again, his love of life and the people around him, as well as his ability to impart these feelings to others is the legacy he has left those of us who were fortunate enough to know him.

All of us here at Westsail want you and all of Dan's family to know that we share your loss and send our deepest sympathy.

Respectfully,

Donald L. McKay

Our newfound friend, Ken, just barely over eighteen at the time, had arrived back in Texas with assistance from long-haul truckers.

"The rage was within me," he admitted. A rage that had been there but had grown more intense after the horror he'd experienced in California.

"I'd always felt like I was runnin' from the Grim Reaper, stayin' just two steps ahead. My time with Dan only magnified that feelin'. My relationship with alcohol was already far less than healthy, and my rage took flight with more abuse. I call it my whiskey years."

He kept busy trying not to think about things too much, staying numb. He jumped from job to job to pay for his boilermakers, which he started drinking earlier and earlier in the day.

"I don't think I was an alcoholic, but I was teetering on the edges of being one."

He was married within a year of returning from California and divorced sixty-one days later. It was two-plus years of sheer craziness, in his eyes.

"Around the same time as my first marriage, me and an older work friend headed down to Soñora, Texas and then on to Cuidad Acuña in Mexico. It was fast livin' lookin' that Grim Reaper square in the eyes. Jack and I ventured down to Mexico a bunch of times together over a couple of years. I'm surprised I went back after the first time. That first trip, I ended up on my knees with Federales' pistols three inches from my forehead. We spent the night in a jail that was worse than anything you can imagine. The drinking fountain was right above the toilet, a hole in the floor. I tried not to use either.

"They had towed and impounded my half-ton Chevy pickup after we were pulled over. I think I drank a fifth of Seagram's all by myself that night. I even hopped a fence at 3 a.m. tryin' to steal my own truck back with my extra set of keys before they put us behind bars. That's when I ended up on my knees, hands behind my head, surrounded by guns. We were about as crazy as two drunk Americans crossing the border looking for nothing but trouble could be. The incident with the police that night all started when I ran an ALTO sign. Hell, I didn't know what ALTO meant.

"I loved rodeo. I loved ridin' bulls. But I never thought about ridin' again after I got home from California in 1974. I don't even have any idea what happened to the bowling ball bag with my bull riding gear."

Sunday Morning

We had been at the THE SHACK for hours: talking life, telling stories. Vicki had delivered me a couple more beers, which helped buffer hearing details I'd never heard before. Loretta had nursed another beer, and Ken hadn't had but maybe a few sips from the margarita. He drank water the rest of the time.

It was pushing 9:00 p.m. Time to wrap things up and get back on the road to Dallas. I felt we had already overstayed our welcome, and we had certainly taken up enough of Ken's time. He must be exhausted, I thought. I was surely whipped.

We paid our tab with Vicki and exited THE SHACK, climbed into Ken's truck, and headed back to Abilene. All three of us were done with the recorder, especially Loretta. At Abuelo's, we said our goodbyes with promises to stay in touch.

Leaving Ken that day was like that proverbial favorite song. You have a letdown when it's over.

It had been a good day, a culmination of a year's long exploration, and a deep dive into details surrounding my brother's life and last days.

Loretta drove us back to Dallas. We were silent for most of the drive, quietly mulling over the day with Ken and his story—a more unabridged version than the one we had known for years. I had wondered about these details for most of my life. It was October 2. I closed my eyes while

Loretta drove and imagined the harrowing events Ken Robinson, the hitchhiker, the young budding bull-rider, went through thirty-six years ago.

We awoke early that Sunday morning and walked the mostly empty streets of downtown Dallas. Even though I had started my career with a Dallas-based company and had traveled to the area numerous times, I had never visited the Book Depository or the Grassy Knoll. My corporation had arranged all my previous trips to Dallas, so I had never explored the city beyond the airport, meeting rooms, and corporate team-building events.

I was four when President John Kennedy was assassinated in 1963. For many my age, that event is one of the first images they can remember from their childhood. I recall descending the stairs after a nap in the Diamond Lake house to find my mom teared up in front of our black-and-white television as the caisson carrying the flag-draped casket made its way down Pennsylvania Avenue. How quickly the world can change, even our own little worlds.

Loretta and I started at the memorial one block east of Dealey Plaza then continued to the Grassy Knoll and the Book Depository. The memorial consumed an entire city block. It was surrounded by Main, Record, Commerce, and Market streets. The epitaph, etched in granite, ended with, "It is not a memorial to the pain and sorrow of death, but stands as a permanent tribute to the joy and excitement of one man's life." The same could be said of this book.

Dan had a great life, and, in the end, he lived as he wanted, breaking norms and the bounds of parental and societal expectations. Fathers and sons will have their conflicts—Dan and my father had their run-ins. Vietnam and the changing times in America made their differences more intense.

My parents passed long ago, freed from the burden of guilt they senselessly carried following Dan's murder. The only humans who should bear guilt over Dan's death are the two men who pulled the triggers of their shotguns in the Mojave Desert that morning. Having said that, I assume they are incapable of remorse, if even they still walk this earth.

I had wondered about the hitchhiker for thirty-six years. I no longer had to wonder who he was or what he may have known. I no longer had to speculate about what kind of man he was, had become, or if he was still alive. I learned how he had come to be in California and that he shared Dan's desire to leave California. Finally, I learned how Ken felt about my brother, Dan, even all these years later.

I've learned more detail about where and how my brother's life ended prematurely, but we'll likely never know why.

Until his own premature death at fifty-five, my father never stopped searching for answers. Could he have somehow stopped it from happening? If he hadn't come home from Chef Carl's that night and lost his temper, would things have turned out differently? If he'd only resisted opening Dan's mail from the US government as he was leaving for Europe, would Dan be alive? Had those tense moments driven his son away from home? Was he somehow responsible?

As for Dan, if he had only … what? There are times when I have wished, "Gosh, if only Dan had gone to Vietnam." To me, it really is the irony of all ironies, the way Dan died after being spared the violence and sadness of the war. Even if he had died in Vietnam, it would have been preferable to what happened on the side of the road in the desert that night. It was only a passing thought a few times in my life. It is so foolish to play those games.

I excavated from storage the harpoon Dan picked up in New England in August 1970, the sword from Toledo, Spain, and the bayonets from France he acquired during his trip in 1972. We've displayed them prominently in our home. Those items now also remind me of Ken, his story, his brief journey with Dan, and his feelings toward a young man he no longer considers a stranger—a person he credits with saving his life.

In subtle ways, Dan was a hero and has been a guiding and protective spirit for me. I'm glad I found someone who felt as I do in Ken.

Newspapers covering Dan's murder used the headlines, "One Last Good Deed Cost Daniel A. Walker Jr. His Life" and "Murder Victim Was Always Doing Favors." This research allowed us simply to give Dan credit for being where Ken needed him to be that October 1, and for being a good, kind, human being.

There is no memorial for Dan, save for a small plot next to my parents in a place not called home for over forty years. There is no marker in the Mojave commemorating his loss. Dan was a budding photographer, writer, and fearless traveler. He died before he could combine those interests into a body of work. Perhaps he would have written stories and put his name on a book. Still, here's hoping Richard Menzies was right in saying that Danny Walker now lives forever.

Danny Boy

A Blog by Richard Menzies
September 29, 2011

I've never been anyone's role model, except once. His name was Danny Walker and he came from an upscale suburb of Chicago to Heber Valley, Utah, where I resided in a distinctly downscale one-room cabin without running water or bathroom facilities. At the time I was working as a lifeguard at The Homestead Resort, and my only possession worthy of envy was a 305cc Honda Superhawk motorcycle.

Danny was visiting his pal David, also from Mundelein and son of a part owner of the resort. In any other time, in any other place, our paths would never have crossed. But in the summer of 1968, it turns out we had quite a lot in common.

See, I had recently given up on climbing up the socio-economic ladder—in fact, I was on my way down that ladder. And Dan, in spite of all his family connections, and to the dismay of his parents, was determined to go the same way. Why? It's hard to explain to people nowadays. I guess you just had to be there.

What Danny loved was not being under his father's thumb. He loved not having to please his mother. He loved the wide-open spaces of Utah and the fresh mountain air. He loved freedom! And he dreaded the future that awaited him as a freshman business major at St. Norbert College. In short, he dreaded the prospect of growing up.

That's when he found me, a grown man who evidently refused to grow up. I was the Peter Pan of Heber Valley, cheerfully doing a boy's job for minimum wage and not the least bit concerned because other than a $30 a month motorcycle payment, I had no overhead.

Danny said he wanted to be just like me, but of course that's easier said than done. Writers don't need to grow up—in fact, it's better that we stay young. For as long as possible, anyway.

We two spent a lot of time poolside, he posing existential questions as I dispensed wisdom from atop my lofty lifeguard perch. When did I decide to drop out of society? he wondered. Did I do drugs? Did I drink?

I didn't do drugs, nor did I drink much. And I refused to buy liquor for Dan or Dave or any of my teenaged coworkers. I knew their parents would certainly not approve of me leading their children astray.

"Oh, puh-leeze," Danny would plead. "You have no idea how hard my life is. My parents are so strict. They're planning to send me to St. Norbert. I need a drink."

Danny likened St. Norbert to Pencey Prep, and himself to Holden Caulfield. At other times, he went by the pen name Phoenixious Jones, or "Finny." On college orientation day, Finny became seriously disoriented after consuming three-fourths of a bottle of Seagrams whiskey.

In a letter dated "sixteen days until freedom" Danny reported that "Finny has sobered up and has quietly fitted back into the society from whence he came (much like Professor Lidenbrook back from his Journey to the Center of the Earth). Once again in suit coat and tie, Finny attends school and is waiting for the end of school.

"Richard, this may sound weird, but I long to philosophize with you alongside a pool. At work, at school, at home, I hope to turn around and see you and talk and joke and verbally scrutinize the Heberites. See ya in July!"

So it came to pass that Dan and I linked up again in 1969 or thereabouts. It's been so long now that I scarcely remember. By '69 I had become romantically involved with Anne, and it had become clear that whatever the future held, I most likely wouldn't be lifeguarding and living in a one-room shack. Still, Dan was determined to follow in my footsteps, and now his letters were sounding less like Holden Caulfield and more like Jack Kerouac. He announced that he was turning his back on St. Norbert College in Wisconsin and had applied to the University of Albuquerque.

"And if accepted I will be only about 500 miles from beloved Heber Valley. If something happens to screw up my plans I will go someplace in Illinois or to St. Mary's College in Minnesota. The main reason I say this is that my parents don't especially want me to go to Albuquerque. I'm so sick of school and my parents—not because they're not good to me but because I'm tired of them having to take care of me. God, I wish I was older! About 21 and just stagnated there or whatever you do to make time stand still."

But time does not stand still. By 1970 Annie and I were living in the city and, having failed in our attempt to build furniture out of papier-mâché, were contemplating the purchase of a sofa. Dan, meantime, had bought a motorcycle and now his letters came postmarked Denver.

"The other day I was reflecting on the possibility of the world starting again in frontier days-the untamed country and all that stuff. I soon realized that the only way this could happen to me was to go to some unpopulated part of the country or world. Looking on the map I found—Australia! It has a vast area in which there is less than one person per square kilometer. That means there must be acres of land that no people occupy."

Meantime, in order to transport the new sofa to our apartment, I had bought a van. Soon as Dan heard that, he bought himself a van. It was in that van that his young life abruptly came to an end. Somewhere in the West, I don't recall exactly where, Danny had pulled off the highway in order to catch some shuteye, and during the night someone had come along and shot him for no reason whatsoever. I have deliberately avoided learning the gory details, except that I understand his killer has never been caught and that Dan's last words, according to an ear witness, were "Don't shoot me!"

Forty years later I think of Dan occasionally and especially whenever I visit Heber Valley, which no longer looks the same as it did those magical summers. Snake Creek no longer meanders freely and the open fields we knew are covered with houses. My cabin is long gone, and so is the wild and crazy horse we called Blaze. Danny loved Blaze and, unlike me, wasn't afraid to ride him. Fast and furiously he rode across the open meadow toward wherever it was that a bright young man madly in love with life might "reach the age of twenty-one and just stagnate there or whatever you do to make time stand still."

rdmenzies.com

Request

Regarding the man named Sam or two men traveling east from Southern California on Interstate 40 in early October of 1974: Sam told a witness they had bought a gold GMC or Chevrolet van in Whittier, California. The same witness was led to believe the two men were following an ex-wife or girlfriend and a child to Indiana. If you have any information, please contact the San Bernardino Cold Case team at (760) 956-5001.

Acknowledgments

As a first time, and likely last time writer handcuffed with creative insecurity and the thought of sharing this very personal and emotional journey of our family with—perhaps the world, there were key figures who stepped in to keep my process moving.

Richard Menzies,

You have now mentored both Dan and his younger brother forty-six years apart. Through 2019, the easy part of this story formulated, but it wasn't until I contacted you that it all started coming together. Your humor, subtlety, and knowledge, not to mention your bond with Danny Walker brought this all together. Your encouragement was invaluable. This book doesn't get written without you.

Tim O'Donnell,

As I could only expect, you were the motivational tip of the spear, pushing and advising from the very beginning. If there is anyone in my life who lives fearlessly, and by Dan's words: *"Limitations. there really are none. Only the one's we put on ourselves,"* it is you. This book doesn't get written without you.

Loretta,

Long before 2009 and up to this moment, you've had the genuine interest in this story that helped resurrect my interest. Your patience, help, encouragement, and behind the scenes research over the last few years has been a contribution beyond measure. Also, "The Project" may have stayed in the can if you hadn't acted as my operations manager and shouldered the continued research beyond the act of writing. I love you! This book doesn't get written without you.

To those we interviewed, so many years ago.

Thank you for your time. I felt a personal responsibility to produce something and honor the time you gave us. Sorry it took so long. This book doesn't get written without you.

And of Course, thank you Ken Robinson. This book doesn't get written without you.

Doug Walker and Ken Robinson at Ken's favorite fishing hole. June 9, 2021

www.ingramcontent.com/pod-product-compliance
Lightning Source LLC
LaVergne TN
LVHW041700060526
838201LV00043B/511